PUZZLED TO
PURPOSE

Excellence Is Never Achieved by Accident

TASHA HART

Printed in the United States of America

ISBN 978-1-948270-22-9
Keen Vision Publishing, LLC
www.keen-vision.com

DEDICATION

*I dedicate this book to my sons, Jeray and Honest –
mommy loves you and I pray you find your purpose
in God and start that journey at an early age.*

*Jordan Hart – You are smart and beautiful inside and
out!*

*To my best friend and spouse Chad Hart – Thank you
for taking the risk with me and supporting me in all
my adventures in Christ!*

*For anyone that finds a connection to your purpose, I
dedicate this book to your triumph and rejoice with
you always!*

Table of Contents

Introduction

It's just a white house on a corner lot in a small town. It has the character of an old man whose face is weathered from years of working in the sun. The handmade wooden steps groan with every visitor that makes use of them. Trees have always surrounded the lot on which this house sits. To me, the trees were
my white picket fence and behind them I played.

The small white house sits among other small homes tangled through quiet streets and regular people living regular lives. The adults spend their days working. They take off each morning in their cars or public transportation and in some cases just a bicycle to get around town. It is during this time "our time" the kids take to back alleys and playgrounds, allowing imaginations to shape the day. It's funny how you can live with a thing or have a thing and not really know you have it. I'm speaking of my imagination now. As a child, I had a vivid and active imagination . I climbed trees and pretended the birds knew my name and waited for me everyday to tell them about my ventures down the alley. I spent many summers visiting family and found myself on an adventure every single day. I didn't know at the time that God would use this skillful tool to show me things. God would sharpen my imagination and use it to reveal things to me. Vision is sometimes described as a thought, concept, or object formed by the imagination. Let me tell you, God has formed many visions within my imagination beginning with a simple thought.

Those back alleys and playgrounds are where I learned to play and use my great imagination. I was a born leader. I always had the sense and creative motivation to bring others along with me during my "adventures". It never took much convincing for others to follow. I loved to play games and anything that involved being around other people--both children and adults alike.

I found people to be like my own personal discovery. There was the man across the street from the old white house I speak of who had a fenced in yard. He had dogs, Dobermans to be exact, and lots of them. Walking passed his house was an adrenaline rush every time my cousins and I ventured to the local park. The thought of those dogs getting out was always in the front of our minds as we went passed.

I remember the day they actually DID escape the prison of their fenced yard. I never knew how fast I could run until that day. Later in high school, I would join the track team and I would think about those dogs as I ran the fifty-yard dash.

I did a lot of walking down those streets in that small town. Passing houses that seemed to age right along with their owners. I didn't know street names, just which house was where and next to what.

I would walk and speak to whoever was on the porches or in the yard. You never passed an elder without speaking. That was considered rude and it would surely get back to your parent or guardian before the streetlights came on. I always spoke and answered with a "yes sir" or "yes ma'am" when I was asked a question.

As I am recalling these people and those streets, many people's faces come to mind. I would have to write several books to explain how they all impacted my life. There was the lady at church who always seemed like if you hugged her too hard, she would break. Her dark cocoa skin was one of the darkest I'd ever seen as a child, but her eyes were kind and she always had candy! I LOVE CANDY! She would have a red cinnamon candy for me or a butterscotch, which she knew were my favorites. I didn't know that my fondness for her would encourage me to be that kind of person toward children when I got older.

This small church was right around the corner, within walking distance of the little white house. I loved the lady with the candy and cocoa skin. I loved the piano playing and all the people at that church that helped shape me into who I am today. God allowed me to be a kid in His presence during those moments at church. I was baptized as a child in that church. I learned how to play games and occupy myself in that church when Pastor would go on with one of his long sermons. My thoughts would travel to what I would do after church when I got back to the little white house on the corner. I could not get enough of hide-and-go-seek or freeze tag. This only occurred when my cousins came by and there were enough of us to play. Most of the time it was just my grandparents and I in this little white house. Being that I spent many summers with my grandparents, I was taught to play games that didn't require as much "energy". I remember my grandmother teaching me to play jacks with the little six-pronged metal pieces and a bouncy red ball. My grandmother was really good and I never once had beaten her in that game. None-the-less I still loved to play with her, win or lose.

As I got older, I was introduced to activities that would occupy my curious little mind for longer periods of time. I believe this happened as a natural parenting technique in order for the adults to get some "Peace & Quiet" (rather than their true concern for my intellect) but once again, I loved adventure! It was during the peace and quiet time that I was placed in front of many books, paper and crayons or one of my favorite puzzles. Although I enjoy all of these activities, it is the puzzle I want to focus on. It's amazing how God will rewind time and bring you back to the simplest memories and turn them into profound revelation for your life. I began this book after asking God some questions about my life, wondering what purpose some of my past experiences would serve. I did what I think most people do as they get older. They begin to feel a sense of urgency more than ever to find the place they fit perfectly in the body of Christ.

You may have had some successes here and there, some experiences, yet you may still (like myself), ask what is my purpose? Where do I fit into the big picture? Like me, you may have asked yourself after a church function, a Bible study, a great Sunday sermon, will this help me help someone and bring us both closer to God? You may have thought to yourself that you are bored with just accumulating more knowledge about the Kingdom of God and not having the opportunity to actually be a true contributing, participating member in it!

With all of this built up frustration, I went to God with one question— really a declarative statement. "Father, I am puzzled about my future. Help me find where I fit." It wasn't in those exact words but that was my heart's cry. He answered me. His answer to my partial statement and question was simply, "Examine your heart". This book will not be going into the actual steps to examining your heart, however, there are many resources on the subject and I do recommend you do that before you attempt to delve into what this book truly has to offer.

I suggest "Battlefield of the Mind" by Joyce Meyer and the up-and-coming writing's of Debbie Miller who attacks the source of heart bondages through her testimony. Debbie Miller takes a unique approach when it comes to breaking bondages and addressing spiritual heart damage. I encourage you to research Debbie Miller and her practical steps on how to break those bondages with instruction from the Holy Spirit.

How I was raised and the small town life I was shaped in has been both an advantage and disadvantage for me in my walk with God. I have many things I can look back and say were triumphs, but yet I have many areas of failure as well. Who doesn't? When God expressed to me that I should examine my heart, I felt a little tug. I didn't quite know what He meant at first. I knew that I loved God and that I sincerely did my best to live for him. My daily goal has been to have a greater impact for His Kingdom.

There were great prophecies spoken over me and prayers of blessing but, that didn't bring me comfort. I had not truly understood the importance of those prophesies and now I had found myself before God being told to examine my heart. Just as the physical heart is used to pump blood throughout your physical body, the spiritual heart parallels that same function. Your spiritual heart is what pumps the life-blood of Jesus Christ through your entire spiritual being. I began to examine my heart and I realized that at some point in my life there were blockages building up in certain areas. Those blockages came as a result of certain experiences in my childhood and on into adulthood. They were keeping the life-blood of Jesus Christ from flowing freely into all areas of my life. I knew that I would have to have spiritual open-heart surgery to remove those blockages and allow the blood to flow properly.

I had never thought about asking myself if I was spiritually fit enough to handle the position God had for me in His Kingdom. Did I have a position? Yes! Did God want me in that position? Yes! I had to get spiritually healthy. I had to examine my heart.

Upon further examination of my heart, I discovered that a lot of the blockages were a direct result of my "good" intentions in life! Many times (because of my unhealthy thoughts) I would attempt to do things I thought were in line with God's purpose for my life based on my idea of what was good. I thought if I could just do more--be more--I would be scooped up into the world of purpose and join the countless other Christians making an impact for Christ!

It wasn't until this heart examination that I realized how God wanted more than my "good" intentions. The heart of a Christian, determines the will of a Christian.

This will of ours has to be more than multiple acts based on good intentions. The true heart and will of a Christian has to be multiple acts of determined obedience. It is our determined obedience to God that eventually drives us to our purpose in life. It is our determined obedience that allows me to make decisions on a daily basis that impact God's Kingdom. If I am determined to get paid in a couple of weeks, I make a decision to be obedient and go to work. If I am determined to have intelligent children, I am obedient and send them to school. The same process happens with us spiritually if want to grow in the knowledge of God we have to be taught. If I am determined to have quality relationships with my spouse, family or friends, I make obedient decisions that make an impact in those areas.

Give God your determined obedience and He will begin to show you your purpose. He will show you how His love has made room for you in His vision for the Kingdom of Heaven. Before you can begin to look at where God wants you and how you fit into His big design, you must first examine your heart. You must realize your intentions may be blockages hindering the life- blood of Christ from flowing. For instance, someone with "good" intentions will participate in a good activity, set up to assist the poor or those in need. Upon further examination they realize they regret it and never really wanted to participate. They just thought it was a "good" thing to do. Perhaps their heart was more into getting recognition for being a participant rather than pleasing the heart of the Father. Some may even participate with the intent of pleasing the Father, but their hearts were never focused on whom they were assisting. They were punching the spiritual time clock and asking the Father to recognize the time they just put in.

Someone with "good" intentions may go out into the world and work a job to gain wealth. That person will say it is for the good of their family that they work long hours and multiple jobs. Now those "good" intentions have those people constantly working overtime and too exhausted to spend time with their family! Eventually, their job becomes an escape and an excuse not to engage the demands of their children or spouse. I know these examples may sound a little harsh, but it is often true whether we admit that to ourselves or not.

Look at the heart of the people in these "example" scenarios. If you only look at the intentions of their heart, you may say they are just good people trying their best. I have heard that statement many times in my life and have often confessed it myself in response to anyone questioning my intentions. Our past hurts and numerous circumstances can cause blockages in the heart. When God expressed that I should examine my heart, I had to realize that this life I live is not about me. Regardless of how the blockages got there or why, I had to make a decision to live in obedience rather than in my idea of "good" intentions. If God was asking me to examine my heart, there had to be a reason and there had to be something I had missed! To find where I fit in God's Kingdom, I had to commit to His vision and allow God to surgically remove the blockages so that the life-blood of Jesus Christ could flow through every part of me.

This spiritual open-heart surgery was a process and it has started me down a path I never expected. With this surgery, the Great Physician brought a lot of clarity in many areas of my life. With the blood flowing and the blockages removed, I could feel myself becoming healthier and stronger to take up my position in Christ. The life-blood of Jesus Christ does not flow to pump out good intentions. How would it feel if Jesus constantly reminded us of all His good intentions, but He never made a decision to commit to the vision of the Father and impact eternity? Where would we be? I knew with this thought, I had to be more like Christ, obedient beyond good intentions into full commitment. Once the examination of my heart was complete, God reminded me that He could keep my heart free from blockages in the future. I would be subject to periodic heart examinations and in turn, He would continue to advise me on healthier decisions that allowed me to stay active with impact for His Kingdom.

I gave God my intentions. Intentions are invisible. Intentions are defined in Webster's New World Dictionary for Young Readers as, "anything planned or purposed." The definition of intent is, "having the mind or attention fixed, concentrating, firmly directed." In the middle of this analogy of the physical and spiritual heart, God explained to me what those blockages were. Again this book is not going to go in-depth about the heart and how to remove those hurts and blockages. There are others very well versed and equipped to deliver that information to you as I have mentioned earlier such as the very well written information on heart bondages by Debbie Miller. For now just understand that the blockages are caused because we confuse conviction with condemnation. They are not the same thing. Conviction pushes us to declare the truth of God and the truth sets us free! Condemnation tells us we are not worthy and we have lost God's approval therefore, no one will approve of us! We have a blockage in one area of our lives or another. Conviction allows us to face the truth and believe our God will loose us with love over the conviction into freedom. Condemnation cuts us off from true connection and fellowship with God and other believers. Condemnation blocks us from the truth by keeping us focused on where we have fallen short.

We may not intend for this to happen but how many of us allowed the flow of God in our lives to stop because of a past hurt? Again, this heart issue has to be addressed FIRST if you intend to move beyond what is blocking you from connecting to your purpose in Christ.

As I gave my intentions to God and allowed Him to remove my condemnation, He reminded me that through the blood of Christ, He had a planned purpose for my life. As the blood began to flow through me again (in areas of my body that had lost spiritual circulation for awhile), I could feel the plans He had for me being directed to all areas of my body concentrating on strengthening me for what I was sent to do.

How do we know if the intentions of the blood are fulfilling the planned purpose it was sent for? When you look at the bigger picture, I am only part of the collective body of Christ. Until this heart examination, I was a blockage to others in the body of Christ because I wasn't allowing the blood of Jesus Christ to flow in all areas of my life! You could tell this was true by the limited positive impact I was having as a member of the body of Christ. I had to get to a place in my life where I realized that it was never about me. As a member of the body of Christ, I was not fully functioning. I was hindering parts of the entire body of Christ from functioning well. Now, God can put in replacements and do some mighty works. He can prescribe things to temporarily fill in where you should be functioning until you are healthy again. I saw all of this. I had to become spiritually heart-healthy in order to properly function in my role of the body of Christ.

You will know you have moved beyond "good" intentions to a fitted and fixed purpose when you can look at the reaction of the Body of Christ and see the "impact"! A healthy spiritual heart pumping blood to the entire body will have demonstration of healthy limbs that are fully active and productive for the Kingdom of God.

I challenge you today to do more than aimlessly find a place to fit into the body of Christ. No! Don't do that! Examine the intentions of your heart, the why behind your decisions, the concentrated purpose of your plans and then choose to fit in where God shows you will have the most impact, based on your unique design and your determined obedience to Him. You were fearfully and wonderfully made, remember?

After God and I went through this heart examination together, it was obvious to me that God only wanted me to be free to do exactly what I had been asking Him for. I wanted to go from being puzzled about my future to being sure about my purpose in Him. I wanted to know that I fit into his "Big" plans for the Kingdom of Heaven! I didn't want to live on the fence of confusion anymore and experience success in Him once in a while sporadically. This is when God began to bring up memories of my childhood and how I had the answer to who and what I was all along! Inside of us are all the unique answers to who we were created to be and what we were purposed to do.

I had heard similar statements in the Christian world before. This time however, my thoughts and desires were leading me down a different path. I was more concerned with finding the heart of the Father rather than seeking my own desires. We are all unique creations of God the Father. There is only one way to the Father and that is through Christ Jesus. However, this is not what this book is about. This book is for believers moving beyond salvation into the depths of purpose. I pray that you see beyond one more book of steps or methods and realize my heart is that of the Father that by sharing some stories, you will relate and God will begin to speak to you in a way that only He can. I can't say what the Father will reveal to you as you read because we all respond to Him in our own unique way. My heart is sincere when I open up to you and ask you to see through my eyes some things the Father has allowed me to see. Our God is an awesome God! SO awesome that He could take a girl from a small town in Indiana, give her an imagination and a passion to share just one more way to go from puzzled to purpose in your life.

Before we can examine the puzzle, it is very important to remember throughout this book that completing a puzzle requires much of the same steps as completing the vision of God for your life. You must first remember to have plenty of workspace to facilitate the activity. Designate an area in your heart for God to begin His work. Now that you have had spiritual open- heart surgery and the blockages are clear, this won't be a hard process. He has already done the hard part. Giving God the space necessary to work is an invaluable starting point for progress in accomplishing

His vision for you. The bigger the vision, the more room you will need in your heart. Have an open heart by which there is room to grow God's purpose.

Chapter One

OUT OF THE BOX

*"When I decided to write this book, I did not forget that
this is an opportunity to share a part of my life with
others. I reflected on that and chose my words carefully
and then at the same time like art on canvas, I just had to
let it all out and allow others to see my work for what it
is...uniquely me."*

Tasha Hart

Stepping out of the box was not hard for me to
grasp in a natural sense. I was that girl that
climbed trees and created a clubhouse out of
wood beams, sticks or whatever else I could find. When
we were young, I used to take my siblings into
abandoned houses to "explore" and see what treasures
someone's interrupted past had left behind. Once we
ventured into an abandoned home that had caught fire
a few years earlier. I don't really remember exactly how
old we all were at the time. I being the oldest child, just
led the pack and on this day when we ventured into the

abandoned home that had once caught fire, the last thing on our minds was safety so brace yourself for the details.

This home was a two story and of course we wanted to get to the top floor. We had peeked in the windows and walked around the vacant home to make sure we didn't see anyone else inside. We came upon a set of broken stairs along the outside of this gray dirty home. After poking around and finding the home to truly be abandoned, we brainstormed on how to get to the top floor. Unfortunately from peeking through the windows, we realized there was no access to the top floor from inside. The home was meant to be a duplex housing unit therefore the upstairs unit would have to be accessed from the outside. The stairs leading to the second floor were damaged from the apparent fire and some of the steps were missing all together. This did not deter our plan to get to the top. Someone had the bright idea of scaling the broken steps, but we won't mention any names.

Scaling the wall along burnt and broken steps until we got to a landing safe for us to stand on, I pushed in the door to the two-story abandoned home. The smell was of old musty carpet and moldy furniture. The home that once probably held a family with memories and moments was left utterly alone. No signs of life had been here for years apart from clothing scattered on the floor, furniture and praying mantises. There were hundreds of these insects everywhere on everything.

They were HUGE and on the furniture, lighting fixtures, walls, and window seals. It seemed as if all their eyes were on us and we had abruptly interrupted their meeting for world domination! They didn't move and neither did we.

I never have forgotten those out of the box moments. God would bring these kind of moments to mind when He wanted to remind me that in all my adventures (through safe and unsafe conditions) He has been there. The more I thought about the abandoned house of mantises, I wondered why I automatically assumed they were having a meeting for world domination. Why not a secret prayer meeting? I chuckle to think about how my mind wonders sometimes but all of this to say, don't be afraid of the adventure ahead! Get out of the box! God is with you in safe and unsafe conditions!

When I was younger, I learned really quickly to look inside the box. It was an exciting game to me where for a few moments you had all the attention in the room while everyone watched your reaction to opening "the box". This wasn't a literal game to be played. It just seemed like a fun game when all the attention was on me. I was never afraid of opening the box. I was actually always on the edge of anticipation and excitement waiting for my opportunity to see what was hidden inside. You may be asking what this has to do with living outside the box? Before you can live outside the box, you will have to explore the contents inside. I was thinking of this exciting game of open the box when God reminded me of the scripture (Matthew 7:11).

Matthew 7:11 NIV

"If you, then, though you are evil, know how to give good gifts to your children, how much MORE will your Father in Heaven give good gifts to those who ask him!"

I realized that my excitement for opening the box (opposed to the fear of the unknown) came from multiple experiences in my past where this scripture (Matthew 7:11) was proven. Over and over again, gift after gift, I was never shocked that the gift inside was good. When I was younger, I was always given "GOOD" gifts! It never failed that whatever the surprise was inside the box it had been especially handpicked just for me! It pleased me to remember that I was fearfully and wonderfully made. My God gives good gifts and we are a gift to God from Himself and it is good! This is how I imagine God views us sometimes--as gifts! We are the carefully selected, handcrafted gift to God Himself for the purpose of fulfilling His vision in love. He enjoys opening the box!

I discovered however, during the course of our lives we have forgotten the gift that we are in God's Kingdom and this causes us to not want to leave the "box". Can you imagine in the middle of this joyous experience, God opens the box and looks inside at the gift we are and our response is "no, I'm not coming out"? The box represents our comfort zone! You may have heard many a sermon on this topic. Getting out of your comfort zone is very important. It is almost instinctive for us to be comfortable. We respond to discomfort differently but a response is definitely required.

Growing up in that small town did not change the fact that I had to do what most children do and that is go to school. Kindergarten was this place that everyone had been talking about for weeks. This buzz over school supplies and new clothes did not make me feel excited. I had no idea what to expect. In this small town we walked a lot. Mostly everything was within walking distance. I had seen this school the adults spoke of. I had passed it on occasional trips to the grocery store and other destinations. It was a huge building in my estimation that swallowed children up by the dozens on a daily basis. They must not have tasted too good because about the same time each day, that huge building would spit them all back out again. The children didn't seem to mind because they allowed this to happen day after day.

I didn't care, the thought made me want to spit something up. I was getting nervous about the big "first day of school"! The building would swallow me up and I would become a part of something, I just didn't know what. Of course I had to go to school and when that day came it was a hopping place of organized chaos. Everyone seemed accustomed to the chaos except me.

I didn't like it and it felt very uncomfortable. This is natural for us as human beings because thinking back on this story, I had already learned what comfort was and wasn't. I knew that being around new people made me uncomfortable. I didn't know any of these people or the children as I was escorted through the huge hallway to my class. I remember once our teacher was instructing the students to come line up at the door. This was a common instruction and the students instinctively followed the teacher's command. In the hustle and commotion, I took it upon myself to hide and NOT get in "line".

We had a piano in our classroom and I quickly got behind the piano when no one was looking. I can't tell you the way a child's mind thinks. I can only tell you that as a child, I was afraid of this place and I hid from it. The teacher took the students off to another classroom for some special experience scheduled for that day. I wasn't interested in anything special. I wanted to go back to what I knew and the comfort of home. As the last of the footsteps left the room and it became silent the thought of my actions began to shuffle through my mind. A few moments later, I heard the teacher come back to the room and in a panicked voice and almost annoyed tone the teacher called my name. I didn't answer. Now something inside me wanted to run out and say "I'm sorry! I was afraid, don't be angry!" Instead, I stayed hidden. I don't know how long this went on but eventually after the teacher's panicked steps had entered the room for the third or fourth time, I purposely made a noise that I knew she would hear. It's funny because I never admitted until now that I made that noise on purpose. I was afraid of getting out of the box into something unknown but the experience of being alone behind the piano, I had another overwhelming sense to be found! I didn't know what to expect in this new world of school but I would face that head on from now on rather than be alone in my "box".

Remembering this story made me realize something I didn't understand before. The need to be comfortable was NOT stronger than my need to belong. I had to come out from behind that piano. I needed to belong.

I've had many experiences since this incident when I was in kindergarten and it is funny how some habits become a regular part of our lives. I can't count how many times God has tried to move me from my comfort zone and I ran and hid. The enemy knows our weak points. There have been times I have been put in uncomfortable positions and because I hadn't gone through my "heart surgery" with God, they created more blockages in my life rather than opportunities for growth further in the body of Christ.

I won't go any further with the issues of the heart. I explained earlier, that's not what this book is about. I only want you to understand that some of the stories were a direct result of how I processed experiences and allowed them to hinder me before I got hold of some truths.

I was saved at an early age. I loved God but yet I still felt empty and lacking in purpose. God brought me this revelation of puzzled to purpose as I was asking myself some serious questions about my future in Him. I now know that moving forward in that purpose requires me to get outside the box of my comfort zone.

Picture the box and its contents inside. It contains multiple pieces. As long as we are all in the box together, it doesn't feel lonely or strange. Look around the comfort zone of your life and be careful as others leave the box, you don't want to be the only one left behind. Those puzzle pieces I'm speaking of represent us as Christians or human beings in general. There are multiple pieces cut into various shapes, colors and sizes, jumbled together, disconnected in a dark space. We are sealed in a box until the day we are exposed to the outside world ready to reveal a vision of God. When it's time to go forward, don't hide--go forward with God.

As a single piece of the puzzle, our view from inside the box can be different from God's point of view. From our point of view, it would be easy to find ourselves getting comfortable with our surroundings inside the box. Maybe this is all there is to my existence, just my single piece of the puzzle. It is important to surround yourself with others who are motivated to move beyond the box as well. Get with people moving in the direction you want to go. There is strength in numbers.

Inside the box it is easy to be deceived into thinking this is all there is to my existence and without a new perspective the deception will continue until you lose all hope of leaving the box all together! The company you keep can help propel you out of the box. I had a choice in that classroom to go with the group and see what was purposed for us that day. My fear of the unknown kept me from that experience and left me alone behind a piano. Again, the box is just a representation of our comfort zone.

I ask you now, when is the last time you left your comfort zone to explore the possible purpose God has for you? Leaving the box cannot be any less scary than remaining in the dark or hiding behind a piano in an empty classroom.

Some things that make you uncomfortable may be just the thing that makes me feel at home and safe. What makes a person uncomfortable isn't as important as looking at how to move past the uncomfortable into a place where you simply trust God. It sounds simple but I can assure you there are many Christians saved and going to meet Jesus just to apologize for not trusting Him with the plans and purposes for their lives. Sometimes the comfort of what we have known or how we have done things before, will keep us from trusting God with what we have not experienced or known. I challenge you today to follow (2 Corinthians 5:7).

2 Corinthians 5:7 NIV
"For we live by faith, not by sight."

Have faith to move from the box into the Father's Presence. He can show you His perspective and begin to move you into your position of purpose. There is a place of trust with God where you simply depend on God from a place of obedience knowing He has a bird's eye view of your situation. Leaving the box will give you the opportunity to see where you fit into God's vision. It will also require all out exposure before God.

As a master puzzler, you would know that upon opening a brand new box full of puzzle pieces, you have to first begin to flip all the pieces over so you can see what you are working with. When we are removed from the box, God begins to flip us face up toward Himself. This takes a lot of trust in God. At the same time, during this process God can begin putting together His vision, sorting all the pieces according to the plans He has for us. I can tell you from experience that leaving the box is never easy. The thought of lying before God (completely submitted to

His vision for your life) is a vulnerable yet freeing place to be. That feeling of vulnerability is common as you are waiting for God to connect the dots. I can remember many such times in my life where this has occurred. The unknown was waiting for me and I had to just trust God that He would piece together my steps, as I remained obedient to His Word.

I've had moments in my life that have pushed me outside the box. Not every outside the box experience is a good one but there are lessons to learn. When I was living near Fort Campbell in Clarksville, Tennessee. I had been trying to find a church home. I've lived in many places and moved around all my life. Moving from Ohio to Tennessee brought many uncomfortable changes including the task of finding a job. I had searched in the paper and through the local career center only to find myself traveling almost thirty minutes to the next town to work at the local drug store. Working in the film-processing department, I had the opportunity to meet many people and share with them in their memories and life experiences through brief conversations over their photos. I would develop film for people trying to gather photos for birthday and wedding celebrations and those commemorating the life of a loved one who had passed. It was during this time I stepped out of the "box" when some things began to happen. Being fairly new to the State of Tennessee, I didn't know what to expect. This was definitely outside my comfort zone.

The results of each moving experience has always given me a new perspective on the people God has created. Coming from the North, I was always taught that blacks were not welcomed in the South and I had to be crazy to move there. These thoughts began to play across the screen of my mind as I found myself fulfilling this new job position in a small town in Tennessee. You might be asking what was so uncomfortable about going to work at a drug store. It didn't take long for me to find out this drug store was not in the friendliest of areas. I was called names by people (not everyone) frequenting the store some of which would not allow me to develop their photos and insisted that I put their things aside for a manager the next day. This made me feel very uncomfortable, as I had not experienced this before. Looking back, I'm sure the enemy was playing on my lack of knowledge about this new place. I was getting rides to work because I did not have a car at the time. One evening after I worked second shift, I found myself stranded with no money. The girl that I worked with that was supposed to give me a ride home did not come in that evening for her shift. As the clock ticked on and my shift came to a close, panic set in as to how my situation was going to work out. I needed my job at the time and I had no family nearby to call or friends to reach out to. I went to work each day in faith that God would take care of me. I was stepping out of my box without even realizing it at the time. It took courage to go to a town you are not necessarily welcome and work those evening hours and not know how you were going to get home everyday but something inside always pushed me passed the unknown.

I was sitting outside the drug store freezing because this was around January. I remember a group of guys laughing at me and making gestures and commenting among themselves about me. I was so embarrassed and it was getting later and darker. All I could do was get up and start walking. I grew up in a small town where that little white house sits on that corner lot and we did a LOT of walking. Walking would always get me away from whatever I wanted to get away from so I walked and walked some more until I came upon this church. I had to climb a hill to get to its front doors, but I hiked it knowing if I could just get to those doors I would feel better. My pace became quicker and I could see there was a light on in the foyer. It was after 10 p.m. and the chances of someone being at the church were slim to none.

As I approached the doors, my hunch was proven correct. There was no one inside the church or on the grounds. Out of pure desperation and some curiosity, I tugged on the metal handles of the door to the foyer. To my absolute surprise the door to the foyer made a slight squeak as it opened up to me. I went inside. The light above the aging red carpet was yellow and dull but bright enough that I felt safe, so I curled up in the corner of that foyer area and decided to go to sleep being that I had nowhere to go and no one to call. No, I did not have a cell phone and during this time pay phones were still pretty popular. The foyer area was a little cold but not nearly as cold as being outside and the floor was hard but I was thankful that I had my jacket to kind of make a pillow and cover myself a little at the same time. I always dress in layers because I'm cold natured anyway. Living outside the box, you never know what is going to happen and this was definitely one of those times. I'm not telling you to go find a job with no true means of transportation or that walking the streets at night is living outside the box. However, what happened next was truly that kind of moment for me. I had barely drifted off to sleep when I woke up to a tall Caucasian man standing over me. I was a little startled but not afraid. I immediately apologized knowing I was trespassing and assumed this man was here to scold me for intruding on the church's property. He had a gentle face with a white burly beard and kind eyes. I almost have tears in my eyes remembering this moment because it was the first time someone in this town had shown me kindness.

The man did not scold me, he proceeded to tell me that he was a member of that church and just so happened to be riding by when he saw me sleeping on the floor. He came to see if he could help me and offered to get me a room for the night at a nearby inn. I graciously accepted not knowing if this guy was serious or playing a potentially dangerous joke. I can only tell you that I've always had a trusting heart and sometimes that has been good and other times not so much. This time was one time it had worked out in my favor. The gentlemen made sure I got checked in and that in the morning I could get home.

Lying across the bed exhausted from the emotional drain, I couldn't believe what had just happened. God saw me and cared enough to send someone to intervene on my behalf. Living inside the box, I would be on my own but outside the box of my comfort, (doing all that I know to do and leaving the rest up to God) He never fails. He answers prayer and will more often than not use someone to connect you to your answer. There is a trust in God that comes when you leave the box! You may not know what is going to happen next but you do know God will be there with you through every bit of your life as you move into your purpose.

Now you might be asking how that experience has changed my life or at this point you might be thinking I'm just stupid for putting myself in that situation in the first place. I can't say that all my decisions in life have been the best ones but God uses them anyway. I learned that in life, I would find people who didn't like me too much because they didn't get outside the box long enough to explore the unknown. Then there are those people that live outside the box and stop by a church in the middle of the night to help a lady in need. I may not know whom or what those circumstances will be but I do know God was strengthening me in an area of trust.

Nothing about your existence will be wasted as you experience life outside the box. I constantly have to remind myself of this vital truth. Every time I forget that powerful truth, I found myself in dark and lonely places without much hope of ever fulfilling my purpose. This is important to note that having these detours in life and various life experiences does NOT remove your place in Christ! It is still there waiting for you to take up your position! You are important to God's vision and He will wait for you. He will guide you and protect you along the way. If you don't get these truths until you are older or beyond the point you feel you should be, remember it's never too late! You will always be on time with God and where God intended you to be.

Today, I am sure of my place and I have accepted the puzzle piece that I am and position I hold in God's vision for my life. I discover daily how these life experiences with God have brought me closer to God. With that in mind, I know my position in Christ is vital to the overall vision for the church and your position is too. My desire is that as you continue to read, you will have a sense of urgency to push all doubt aside and allow God to take you from your comfortable box and begin to move you into your purpose. You will gain insight regarding what it takes to be strengthened in your inner man to handle your position, but first you must be willing to leave your comfort zone. I do mean YOUR comfort zone and not what someone else believes to be your comfort zone. Others can detour you with their good intentions by giving you what kept them from fulfilling their purpose. That is not my goal. Your box may not look like mine but I guarantee you have one. If you haven't left it or you find yourself going back to your box when times get tough, it's time to LIVE outside that box of your comfort. Make a decision to permanently trust God for the vision He has for you. You know what that thing is that sends you hiding behind the piano and back to the box. Place it openly before God, allow him to deal with it and then remember you are a vital piece to the vision of God and you are not alone.

What would the final result of a puzzle be if there were pieces missing? God thought so much about each and every one of us that He gave us a place in His Kingdom. What are you waiting for? If you believe that you play a vital role in the vision of God for His Kingdom – you are a piece of the puzzle. It's time to get out of "the box".

Chapter Two

MY PIECE

"I've always enjoyed helping others and God has shown me that it is in the little things I do everyday that help others in a big way."

Tasha Hart

When I spoke earlier of the box, I introduced you to the idea that you are a vital piece of the puzzle I'll call, God's vision. If you think about an actual puzzle it takes time to place all the pieces together to finally get a view of the overall picture. I think of our purpose in God's Kingdom in this way. He places all the pieces together. He knows what the picture will look like. You have a purpose that is unique to whom God created you to be. You were not created "AFTER" the fact or "AFTER" the vision as a back up plan. YOU were apart of the original plan, the original design, the original vision, and the BIG picture. You have a purpose so let's explore the piece you are a little closer. A master puzzler doesn't begin a puzzle without first having all the pieces ahead of time.

When I was younger, I didn't have to think much about my part in my family. My parents divorced when I was around the age of eight, so my role as the "oldest" daughter became that of second caretaker to my mother. When my mom wasn't around, I was in charge. Looking back, I can laugh and say this is where my strength as a leader was born. I had to learn to keep my siblings occupied, entertained, fed and safe all at the same time. This was not easy! I also had to sometimes include the personalities of my younger cousins into this equation as well. I became comfortable with this role because it was never impressed upon me to doubt my position. I wasn't given a long speech about how the house could burn down if I let the hot dogs boil over. I wasn't asked any questions regarding my confidence level or how I felt about the responsibility of the situation. No, it was implied that I had the confidence and could handle the responsibility and more importantly I was needed! No one seemed to care that I was only eight or so, so I didn't care either.

I am amazed when I think that over time, the only thing that has changed my mind about who I am and what I am capable of is ME! Yes, there have been other influences in my life that helped me to shape that mindset, but ultimately the decision was mine.

As an adult, I changed from believing I could into believing I couldn't. God has never questioned my identity or my capabilities! I never questioned my confidence, my identity or what my capabilities were until someone else did! As you get older in the world, you are told more often that you can't do this or you can't do that especially if you are not serving in someone's personal need of you. Simply put, most people are very confident in your abilities when they need you. Looking back, I know now that I wasn't afraid of a challenge or stepping up to new responsibilities as long as it was confirmed that I was needed and what I was doing served some purpose.

My greatest fear became not being needed and therefore without acceptance and purpose, at least from the world's stand point. This isn't anyone particular person's fault. It became apparent that out here in the real world, out of the box, I had people in authority over me who had learned this way of thinking and decided to groom me in the same thought process.

The day I came out from behind the piano was one of those moments. Rather than recognize the fear of a child and all my anxiety about this thing called school, the teacher was fraught with the distress over my brief disappearance and the fact that I did not follow the rules. Very understandable! She had to clue me in on the dangers of not complying, not falling into "line." My teacher had been trained in the ways of the world and what she could and could not do.

I began to look at life through a lens filled with rules and impossibilities and most of all fear. The rules became similar in most settings from school to work. Do your best and if possible, beyond your best. Make me proud, make me look good and above all else, don't get out of "line"! This world was NOTHING like the one I grew up in.

I know what its like to daydream and be snapped back to "reality" by the sound of a bell. The ringing of reality sounded off every hour or so during my years of schooling. Off I went to the next stage of my life with a job and so forth. With a job there were never any bells ringing, but the sound of clocks ticking and the same business of organized chaos. The buildings were taller but they still had the task of swallowing people up and spitting them out on a routine basis. I eventually became comfortable with the rules. I knew that teachers liked it when I raised my hands so I did that often. I learned that if you cleaned up after yourself the janitors would appreciate your generosity and sneak you crackers from the cafeteria. I learned that if you could mush all your food together and swallow it with a gulp of chocolate milk to wash it down you earned the right to sit with the cool kids! I learned to run faster, jump higher and climb trees better than any girl my age. I learned if I donned the title of tomboy that no one would really bother me. As I got older, I knew that good grades kept me from being grounded and allowed me moments of freedom. There were those extra projects at work that earned me the title "Employee of the month". I've collected these titles along the way in this journey called life.

None of these titles of compliance however were grooming me to understand who I was in Christ or how important I was to His Kingdom! I STILL had to come to a point in my life where I had to have more. I had to find out where I belonged! There were all these new things that people were telling me I was and that it was a good thing. As I advanced in following the rules and staying "in line" it became increasingly hard to see what good my unique and individual role in life truly was. I was good at doing what I was told was good but I didn't feel like I mattered or that I had much impact beyond a few pats on the back for staying "in line". Inside, I felt like although I was good at making my existence beneficial for those around me, tt didn't make my existence beneficial or good for the Kingdom of God. I was created to be more than just good at following the rules and meeting people's expectations.

This deep sense of emptiness grew within me as I grew up in the world. I didn't know where I fit or where I belonged but I was figuring out how to blend in until I got some answers.

You could say I eventually earned the title of Master Chameleon. If it was younger children, I could play hopscotch with the best of them, invent a game, play hide-and-seek, which I still do to this day and the kids instantly accept me. With the teens, I could come up with the latest sound, create a rhyme, talk the talk, and walk the walk so to speak. My elders enjoyed conversations of how things used to be while engaging the comforts of their memories like knitting. I learned to knit and have gone down memory lane with the sweetest people! Growing up in that small town with the little white house on the corner, taught me to relate to people! I had to because it was our way of life.

You spoke to everyone and they spoke to you. I knew what to say to Ms. Delores down the street. A middle aged woman who made me cream peas one day because I told her I had never had them at my house. We would sit on her porch with her little black poodle Pepper. I didn't like Pepper much because he barked constantly and I had to speak a little louder than normal to get Ms. Delores to hear me. She told me stories about her childhood, showed me pictures of her kids and relayed to me where they all were living at that time. I loved her stories and my imagination would take me to the places she described. I did this often and everywhere I moved with my mother. I became good at starting new schools and blending in with the new kids. That's funny that I call them "new" when actually I seemed to always be the "new" piece of the puzzle, trying to find my place. This was and has been my life in general over the years.

The constant movement among people with their traditions, routines always made that yearning to fit in grow stronger within in. I wanted the comforts of fitting in or belonging somewhere. I've met dozens of people and heard stories and seen pictures of places I've never been, apart from my imagination.

There was a woman who lived a few doors down from us when I was in middle school. Her name was Ms. Helen. You always put a Ms. or a Mr. in the front of someone's name unless you were related to them or they were your same age. So Ms. Helen was an older woman in her late sixties who absolutely LOVED Elvis! I loved it when she would talk about a concert she went to when she was younger or when she would bring out all her souvenirs. Ms. Helen had an Elvis stamp collection that she framed and hung on her wall. None of those stamps have been in circulation and I imagine that frame is still hanging on her wall in the exact same location. After school, I would do my homework and chores then it was off to escape in the world of Ms. Helen where she taught me to weave placemats and potholders, all while we watched the Grand Ole Opry.

This would be the beginning of my love for country music. I began to learn line dancing by the time I was in high school and I still have the newspaper featuring my boot scoot boogie technique for the entire school.

Yes, I knew how to blend, how to relate but I still felt completely and utterly alone! That saying about being in a room full of people but I could still hear the crickets, was so true. I still hadn't found my place! I still didn't have a sense of where I belonged. My family moved around a lot. I learned to belong and fit in without really being accepted.

At one point in my life, I remember thinking I had been in the third grade three times but actually I had only transferred schools a lot that year.

I can't be the only one who has spent years with thoughts of wondering question after question. I knew from that little church I was baptized in that I was created. I knew I was saved and I loved Jesus but now what? That is the question. What does God want with a little girl born and raised in a small town in Indiana, with lots of stories, lots of experiences, full of imagination but no real place in the world? Surely the God I knew had more for me? Throughout my life this question would drive me to many more experiences. After my spiritual heart surgery, God began to show me where I had missed it. He gave me this analogy of a puzzle and began to show me how each piece separately and as a whole would give me the answer I was looking for.

I was looking at the "puzzle piece" as an individual and God began to show me some simple but profound revelations. The pieces to a puzzle have similar characteristics just as individual people do. Although each piece is unique and has a shape all its own, there is a similar pattern in its make-up. (2 Timothy 1:13).

2 Timothy 1:13 NIV
"Hold on to the pattern of wholesome teaching you learned from me-a pattern shaped by the faith and love that you have in Christ Jesus."

We are patterned and shaped by the faith and love we have in Christ. My question to you is what does that shape look like? If your faith and love in Christ is shaping you, what do you look like? This may sound complicated but it really isn't. How would you use your faith and what for? Does that image of yourself remind you of Christ? I had to stop right here for a moment and ponder what this meant.

Imagine who you are in Christ. Truly begin to see yourself how God views you. The Word tells you who you are in God's eyes. You are the salt of the earth, the light of the world, a city on a hill, His righteousness, and the bride of Christ. You are made in God's own image. Now look at your own individual characteristics, talents and passions. We are going to look at the shape of a puzzle a little closer. You will find there are portions of the puzzle piece that are cut away from the original shape and portions of the puzzle piece jutting out.

This design of a puzzle piece has certain areas cut away and other areas protruding for a reason. This is part of what makes a puzzle piece unique and perfectly designed to fit in somewhere specific. Just as a puzzle piece is designed with a destination in mind that brings about a perfect fit, so has our Lord designed each one of us.

When we look at how we are designed and if we are resembling Christ, its very important to ask if we are leaving room in our lives for connection? Jesus did. As a single puzzle piece, without connection to other pieces in a puzzle, the intended image does not come to fruition and the puzzle is never complete. Not only that, but without the connecting pieces, an individual piece has little or no value. Its purpose is served when it fits in just where it was designed to fit amongst other perfectly aligned pieces. The same is true for the body of Christ.

Are you leaving room for connection in your life with other believers? How we are shaped and created gives us the ability to find our fit in the body of Christ. It is where and how we will find our purpose. Yes! I'm talking about connection. You will not be able to fulfill your purpose alone and many Christians confuse co-existing with true connection. We are not talking about networking, folks! Connection is much deeper and it is how we will interlock with other people to reach our purpose in the Kingdom of God. To interlock with something is when two or more things engage each other by overlapping or by the fitting together of their projections and recesses.

I found this to be absolutely amazing! You mean to tell me I don't have to blend in. I can stand out and be exactly who I was created to be and somewhere, somehow along the way, I will be used to connect with others. Discovering who you are in Christ through your character, gifts and talents as an individual will allow you to interlock with certain other pieces of God's creation to fulfill a purpose. The part of the puzzle piece you are has a section carved away as well as the part of the piece that is jutting out. Lets focus on one area at a time.

You are open to what God has for you and you are praising Him for moving you in that direction. You have heard a little about connection and now all of a sudden you find yourself facing another step to get to God's purpose for your life. You have to learn how to connect with others in the body of Christ. (Romans 12:4-11) explains – although we are many parts (or in this example pieces to the puzzle) these parts do not all have the same function. In order to get further along in this journey of finding your purpose, you have to also consider the idea that finding your fit in the vision doesn't mean you will know how to function when you get there. Yet, is very clear in (Romans 12) that we do have a specific function.

Romans 12: 4-11 NIV

"For just as each of us has one body with many members, and these members do not all have the same function, 5: so in Christ we, though many, form one body, and each member belongs to all the others. 6: We have different gifts, according to the grace given to each of us. If your gift is prophesying, then prophesy in accordance with your faith; 7: if it is serving, then serve; if it is teaching, then teach; 8: if it is to encourage, then give encouragement; if it is

giving, then give generously; if it sis to lead, do it diligently; if it is to show mercy, do it cheerfully. 9: Love must be sincere. Hate what is evil; cling to what is good. 10: Be devoted to one another in love. Honor one another above yourselves. 11: Never be lacking in zeal, but keep your spiritual fervor, serving the Lord."

It can be exciting when you finally find your fit in the vision! You have come so far since you left your comfort zone, but I caution you not to get comfortable now. There is work to do.

True connection requires true function. I know Christians who find areas they can function but there is no connection however it is rare that I find Christians who have connection that don't function. What do I mean? I can go to work and function on my job but that doesn't me I have connection there. In this scenario, I can do what is expected of me and even excel at my "duties" but that doesn't necessarily connect me to my purpose. On the other hand, I can get involved with something I'm extremely passionate about and the results will be greater than merely functioning; it will be connection. I'll explain further by saying you can become disoriented with the cares of life causing a sense of disconnect. The cares of this world can cause you to be cautious of the connection process all together. Anyone who has ever experienced deception, disappointment or disapproval can attest to this feeling of disconnect. RING THE ALARM! This is a strategic plan of the enemy to keep you from your purpose! The Bible tells us in (1 Peter 5:7) to cast all our care upon Him.

We can't go back to the box, isolating ourselves from our purpose, because we have become burdened with negative experiences in our lives. Our purpose will involve connecting and that is why the enemy attacks us hard in this area to isolate us. Women (especially, during this day and age) rally behind the word independence and there is nothing wrong with that word in and of itself, but as a whole in the body of Christ, we can't afford to lose any pieces to the puzzle. We have to focus on the bigger picture and that includes YOU! The burdens and experiences of our past will tell us this is too risky and a potential threat to our hearts. I can now see after my spiritual heart surgery that with God, there is no risk because I am secure in Christ Jesus. It's not about my past and me, it's about Christ and my future. Let me repeat something, it's NOT only about YOU! It's time to get connected and learn how to function in the place you were created for! Give up your cares and lets move on.

1 Peter 5:7 NIVE
"Cast all your anxiety on him because he cares for you."

This isn't just for your sake. If you are burdened and disconnected, the body of Christ is missing a vital functioning piece of the vision God has for us all. You have to be free to connect with others as God leads you into your purpose. I know how it feels to want to cut yourself off from anything that could potentially hurt you but if you trust God this is almost impossible. God loves people and that is risky business. The issue with not taking a risk is that you risk losing out on those things that could potentially do you good. This is not speaking of abusive or negligent risks that could potentially cause you physical harm. I am speaking of going outside those areas of our comfort and saying, "God, I'm ready to plug into someone else's life, someone else's ministry, someone else's circumstances and trusting and I trust You."

A good friend of mine always reminds me and some other ladies in our church that sometimes, all you have to do to get connected is take your focus off who is pouring into your life and your circumstances. Find someone else to pour into and something of value to plug into because when you are focused on someone else, that gives God room to focus on YOU! This, my friend is where you will find yourself functioning in your purpose. As you begin to find areas to plug in, connect, focus, pour out, pour in, you will suddenly realize God has sent someone to do the same for you. The piece of you that allows you to connect with others is that piece of the puzzle shape that juts out. The puzzle piece has a unique shape and the portion of the puzzle that juts out represents our unique experiences, gifts, talents and knowledge in Christ. When we are open to what God wants and ignore the failures of our past, we can use this part of ourselves to connect to others, pouring hope, confidence and encouragement into their lives through the love God has shown us in ours. We overcome by the blood of the Lamb and the words of our testimony.

Once we are free and comfortable with whom God created us to be, these experiences become opportunities instead of hindrances. These experiences witness to others and help us find purpose from our past. However, if we are unwilling to leave the box of our comfort zone and are unwilling to connect, allowing our past to block our future, we miss our opportunities to connect. It is so true that in others we find the missing pieces to our individual purposes, as do they in us. You never know who is waiting on you to be the connecting piece to their purpose as well. We all have a piece of the puzzle. Just be who God created you to be and watch His vision unfold. There is more to who you are than you think and yes it will require a lot of pouring into others or GIVING of yourself, however it will also be necessary to receive as well.

Now we can talk about that cut out space of your piece of the puzzle. This space is the voided area we so often direct our focus. The area where we selfishly forget about all others in the world and focus on what we want and what we need and what are others going to give us. I'm speaking of this space negatively for a moment because that is how most of us at some point in our lives treat this space. Unfortunately a single piece of a puzzle can't fill it's own void. That sounds funny, but how many of us have been caught doing just that? We were not meant to be solely dependent upon ourselves, constantly fulfilling your own needs. We convince ourselves that we don't need anyone else. We lose our patience with people and we lose our common sense at times. I alone as a single piece of a puzzle can't fill my own void nor can I complete the vision God has for the body of Christ or myself as an individual.

So lets look at this space again from a positive point of view. That space in you is reserved for the right person at the right time that God has ordained to pour into you according to His purpose and His vision for the church. Do you know what that means? That space was not an accident! God didn't leave you with that voided space and no plan of filling it. Are you puzzled yet? I was. I needed to look back on my life for a moment and realize that I had tried to fill this void when many things and various activities both in and out of a Christian setting. All of which were failed attempts to complete a vision and fill a space I did not create. The only one who could fill this space was the Creator Himself. Now let me clarify. We are still speaking about purpose. This voided space cut away from the puzzle shape is simply an area where God will use others to fill a need that furthers you along in fulfilling that purpose in your life. There is a part of you that was only meant for Christ to fill. That part of you is about connecting to and only with Christ our Savior. That goes deeper to the core of who you are not what you were created to do as far as purpose. The idea of connecting to your purpose and fulfilling that area of your life is where we will stay focused for the purpose of this puzzling exploration.

As the Holy Spirit was showing me how puzzle pieces parallel individuals in the Body of Christ, He showed me a puzzle piece doesn't decide where it should be placed. It has a place and should not be moving out of place trying to connect in areas it was not created for. Not only can I not fill my own void, I can't fill a void cut and uniquely carved and filled for someone else.

How often have you tried to connect to that lady or that guy only to find out you did not fit? What about connecting to that job or that position in the church only to find out you don't fit? What about that college or that sports program only to find out you didn't fit there either? You are getting the idea. It became apparent to me; my need to fit in had to be balanced with fitting into the right position created just for me.

It is okay to explore all areas of possibility when you are finding your fit, but many make the mistake of conducting this process alone. Our creator plays a big role in this sorting process. Imagine a puzzle piece taking on a life of its own, and when it views the creator actively working one area of the puzzle it jumped from where it was waiting to be placed, dead center where all the action was currently taking place. The Master puzzler, (knowing the piece didn't belong in this portion of the puzzle) would place the piece to the side in order to go back to it later at the proper time. The piece gets impatient and once again, jumps into another area of the puzzle where the Master puzzler has now redirected His focus. In time, this piece has tried to squeeze into areas it was never meant to fit solely based on the excitement of what was happening in another area. This piece was not willing to wait on the Master puzzler to begin working it into the area it belonged all along. Some Christians can be this way for a lifetime and all this commotion causes frustration and again disconnection.

I have seen this time and time again. The Pastor of a growing church starts updating classrooms in the children's program. There are teachers painting, saw blades hacking, talk of new program materials and exciting new resources to make learning more engaging. I participated in such projects many times. It never failed that the same people who didn't want to watch the children on Sunday in the nursery wanted to be the "new" teacher heading up the nursery program. There would be new faces volunteering to be everything from the children's door greeter to the children's pastor all because it was the "new" thing. These same people would not fit into this program but rather than admit that to themselves they would try to "squeeze" in and make room for themselves in an area of the vision they were never meant to take part. This isn't an absolute truth just merely a warning. Don't be satisfied with just being where the action is; get in where YOU fit in. You will be happier and more importantly you will function properly allowing others around you to do the same.

Think of it this way, while this piece of the puzzle was out trying to make a space for he or she, two things were going on. One, the puzzle piece was occupying someone else's space for the time being. If you are constantly trying to be something you were not created to be, adapting to fit in an area you were never shaped for, you are not only circumventing your own purpose, you could also be the barrier to someone else finding their purpose. Second, while you are getting all bent out of shape trying to fit into areas you don't belong, your space is unfulfilled. There are pieces that were specifically created to connect only through you! Again, a gentle reminder that it is NOT all about you! Could it be you are the missing piece to something God wants to fulfill in someone else's life? Simply put, get your piece in gear! At the right time, the right people will connect to you, and you will find those God has sent to connect to your life will provide all the "new" you never knew you needed.

Take a breath – lets look at this a little closer. I don't want to get to far ahead before you really grasp the importance of one single piece of the puzzle. I have learned over the years how to blend with people as I mentioned earlier, but blending and connecting are two separate things. I could be in a room blending without ever making one true connection. However, I have had several moments of true connection that now I find God using to remind me of some of His spiritual truths.

While living in Ohio, I attended a non-denominational church that was registering students to take theology classes through a college in Georgia. After living in Ohio for some years, circumstances brought me to Tennessee. I had only been taking theology courses at my church for a few months, but I didn't want to discontinue my studies so I searched for the nearest sister campus. The only two campuses were located in Hendersonville and another at a small church in LaVergne, Tennessee. I chose the nearest location to where I lived, which truly ended up being another divine experience for me in my walk with the Lord.

Two years later and continuing with my studies, I had earned my associate's degree and was eager to continue on toward my bachelor's in theology. My passion for teaching made classes fly by and I enjoyed every minute! I'm skipping a lot of details because I believe God will use that information for another subject on another day but for now, let me tell you about one of my professors and what she has to do with this idea of connecting.

Although all of my classes were interesting and taught me a lot, none of them intrigued me like those taught by Dr. Fushia Pickett. This woman in her eighties going into her nineties could teach and preach the socks off any experienced minister and you could say I felt a connection. There are those people and those times in your life you come across a moment when you feel deep in your soul you have met these people before or you have been in that place before but that can't be right. This was how it felt for me attending Dr. Pickett's classes. I loved to hear about her experiences in the Lord and with the Holy Spirit. She made God real to me, and the Holy Spirit even more so! She shared about her Methodist background and how all this excitement in the Holy Spirit was new to her but she longed for a relationship with God the Father, The Son and the Holy Spirit.

I could relate to that craving in my spirit and it excited me that God granted her request. For Fushia, nothing was impossible with God. I have such a respect for her and all that God had shown me through her studies with the Holy Spirit. I remember in one class she taught the presence of the Lord was so strong, the Holy Spirit blew through the room moving papers on all the desks to the floor. There wasn't a fan of any type present in the room and the air wasn't on at this time because it was winter. The way a sister campus works is that you view the instructors on video with your other classmates and a Dean is on site to answer questions and review tests, etc. Since many of Fushia's classes were on video, I had never actually met her in person. Instructors would visit campuses on occasion for graduation ceremonies and such, but I wasn't so privileged to have attended one where Fuchsia was present. Fuchsia and the Pastor of the church that hosted the sister campus for our college studies were good friends and occasionally she would make a visit to the church in person. Coming to the end of her years, Fuchsia was making visits to near friends and churches all over the United States leaving a prophecy for the future generations to come after her.

I was working a full time job at this point (years later after the drug store incident) and I wanted to be at the church to meet Fuchsia in person. This woman whom I had never met in person had made such an impact on my life that I'm still reading her books today and encouraging others to do the same. As I said before, she was coming to speak at the church where our classes were hosted and the evening she arrived I once again had no transportation. Let me remind you that the nearest sister campus to me and where I lived was in LaVergne, Tennessee about 30 or so minutes outside of Nashville. At this time, my car was wrecked and I was not able to make it to the meeting. You want to talk about heart broken? Imagine that your favorite movie star, musician, author, sports player was going to be near you and the ticket price is free to attend but you need a ride to get to the location. That is what this day was like for me. I had a free invitation to meet someone I highly respected. I was missing out on the opportunity to meet her and thank her in person. A friend of mine at that time that I worked with happened to have the evening off with no plans and wanted to cheer me up. Poor pitiful me sitting at the house alone sulking about my missed opportunity decided why not. My friend picked me up and although LaVergne was too far for her to drive and take me to this meeting she thought dinner would be nice to get my mind off of the situation for a while. It worked for a little bit. We decided to go to Olive Garden, one of my favorite places to eat. I wanted to go to the Olive Garden I was familiar with on the opposite side of town, however, my friend decided to go to the not as popular location closer to where we were at the time. I made no fuss about the selection because at this point, I really didn't care. My mind was on all the good things that were going to take place tonight that I'd be missing out on. I tried not to show it and be appreciative of my friend's efforts to cheer me up.

With a smile, a little small talk and giggles over silly things, we arrived at Olive Garden. It was a little more packed than usual and I was surprised that the less popular location had a waiting room full of guests eager to get a table. I offered my friend the opportunity to exit and opt for something quicker with less waiting time, but she knew I liked Olive Garden and decided there was no hurry to get me back home alone again. With that we found two seats in the waiting area hoping there would be a table for two sooner than later.

My friend and I got caught up in conversations tuning out all the other noisy conversation in the room when the doors of the waiting area opened and in comes Fuchsia Pickett. I will NEVER forget this moment for as long as I live. She had a glow about her that made me feel like angels escorted her into the establishment. Pastor Howard (of the church hosting our sister campus) was pushing Fuchsia in a wheelchair. Her hair was gray, thick, and curled around her face to bring attention to her light make up and well put together suit. I was speechless! I understood that statement made in movies "I could not believe my eyes" because it was true. I got to speak with her and tell her thank you for the influence she had on my life.

Fuchsia passed away a week or so later. That church was the last church she spoke at. I told you that story for two reasons. Again to reiterate that God sees us and He cares about even the smallest of things that matter to us, such as meeting someone you admire. The second point I want to make is pertaining to my friend. She did NOT have to pick me up that day. My friend did NOT have to take me to dinner. My friend did NOT have to encourage me to stick around and take some time to just enjoy a friend's company but she did.

She was a vital piece of the puzzle that day and an answer to my prayer. She also was blessed because she could not deny that the moment was an act of God. What were the odds? With God the odds are always in our favor. You have to understand that giving someone a ride, taking them to dinner, offering your kindness, saying a kind word, paying someone's grocery bill, fixing someone's car, giving a hug and the list goes on, can all seem insignificant in the BIG scheme of things, but these things can make huge differences in an individual's life. I want to offer you a different point of view. God's point of view is so much higher and above our ways. Lets look at (Ephesians 3:20).

Ephesians 3:20 NIV
"Now to him who is able to do immeasurably more than all we ask or imagine, according to his power that is at work within us,"

This means there is nothing God can't do! The key to this scripture is understanding that word "you" in this scripture, includes YOU. Sometimes I think as believers or people in general we read things and automatically take the back seat and say that it is for someone else. You have to believe that you are a vital piece to God's greater visions and purposes in life. Something you do or have done may be viewed as insignificant to you, but in actuality it is a vital piece of the puzzle connecting God's vision, one person, one prayer and one piece at a time. If you believe that and you want to explore more about how you "fit" into this puzzle, I dare you to keep reading.

The acts of a friend and many experiences with God through connecting with people has gotten me further in fulfilling my purposes in God than any single thing I've ever done alone. This process of connecting is done through everyday choices. I could have decided NOT to go to dinner with my friend. I could have decided to stay home and not connect. I could have NOT casted my cares upon My Lord and Savior and sunk my chances for having a great experience with God that has forever changed my life.

The power of connecting is sometimes moving passed that fear of letting someone in too close. It is allowing someone into that cut out space of ours. It is here God does some real life- changing work. This process of connecting interlocks our puzzled existence with our purpose. As God begins to move us around, we will find places we fit.

Chapter Three

BOUNDARIES

"I have watched plants grow. I believed in the seed that was planted. I know that I can achieve whatever my heart truly believes in."

Tasha Hart

This chapter is going to challenge us to explore our boundaries. This is different from our comfort zone.

Let me explain a little bit of my own history with this area. We moved a lot in my childhood and one of those moves placed me smack dab in the middle of one of God's most beautiful backdrops. The mountains of Pennsylvania and Maryland were my back yard for most of my high school experience.

Moving from Indiana to a small town in Pennsylvania was another "fitting in" process for me. It wasn't going so well and by the time I hit high school, I had decided enough was enough and I would do whatever I could to find a comfortable place to exist. Take the anxiety of being a teenager; add moving to another unfamiliar and uncomfortable place and the fertile ground for trouble awaited me.

My mother being a single mom of three had pretty strict rules. One of which was no hanging out after eleven o'clock no matter the event or the day of the week. This was okay until I realized that I was one of the few teenagers my age that had this kind of curfew. Most of the teens my age had parents still acting as teens themselves and therefore they did not care too much about giving their children boundaries. I understand my mom's boundaries now, but at the time it just seemed unfair. Those Mondays after the weekend all the popular events that took place would be discussed in detail around lunch tables and in between classes. These conversations that caused so much excitement followed by laughs or gossipy whispers were Greek to me because I was never there to experience them!

Okay, this is where you feel sorry for me right? Poor child who had a mother that cared. I know what you're thinking. I was a teenager who just had to see what was on the other side. One night I decided not to care about the rules and see what all the excitement was about. I wanted to be a part of the conversations that would take place that Monday at school. I could picture myself whispering about the latest and greatest and I would be able to genuinely laugh about whatever had happened and know why it was hilarious.

That whole week prior to my "escape" into freedom the school was buzzing with conversation about a party at a friend's house. Of course the parents would be gone for the weekend and the plan was set for a night of...hmmm? A night of what exactly, I didn't know! That was exactly my point. I wanted to know. When you lose sight of where God has placed you, it's easy to think you are supposed to be somewhere else.

My mind was racing with ideas of how I was going to get to the destination of fun. My mom had me on a curfew remember? How was I going to get beyond the boundary? Understand that my mom was no Mrs. Cleaver and punishment would not be light if I crossed this boundary. I don't know what I was thinking when I decided that crossing this boundary would have to be a permanent decision. There would be no going back! That's right folks; I decided that in order to participate in this once in a lifetime event, I would have to run away!

No more hearing about the great adventures that took place over the weekend on Monday mornings at school. No more phone calls from friends with giggles in the background explaining to me that I was missing out.

I was a teen and so forgive me for not thinking about where I would sleep, how I would eat or how my siblings would get in the house after school with me gone. It was all about me and off I went! I had lied to my mom and explained I was going to take out the trash. I had a garbage bag full of clothes and calmly walked out the door. That's right! Me, and a trash bag of clothes went out the door. My heart was racing as I got close to the dumpster in our neighborhood. Quickly passing the dumpster, I ran. What was I thinking? I didn't have time to think! The thought of my furious mother was enough to make me run faster! Those fifty-yard dash practices were coming in handy as I made my way to the intended destination.

When I arrived at the party, I left my bag of clothes outside on the porch so not to draw attention to my recent act of defiance. It was evening by now and dark outside. Just as described the parents of this home were gone and the house was full of teens from school. A popular movie had just come out and we were watching it on the VCR. Oh, yes, the VCR was in play and teens were laughing. I was there. I was in the crowd and I was not going to miss out.

I have always been an eccentric person and that came back to haunt me during this special occasion. Even when I tried to fit in, I was standing out. I was there and I was with the "right" people but something wasn't right. One of the most popular guys in school, a senior, came up to me and asked to speak to me outside. I thought cool, he is going to tell me how cool it is I made it and maybe share some cool secret that only the "cool" kids are privy to. I remember standing outside that door, looking through the screen at all those teens watching the movie and the popular guy in school standing outside with me beginning to give me a lecture. WHAT? Are you kidding me? A lecture, coming from the leader of the misfits! I was almost devastated to the point of tears! All this time I plotted to get to the other side just to be rejected!

Looking back it amazes me that when you are set apart, there is nowhere you can run or hide. God will see you and even the "other" side has no place for you. I remember it like it was yesterday. The "ring leader" of the misfits gave me a warning. I was okay to stay for the night, but I could not stay out with that group of kids. He told me that I was different and if I didn't go home, he would call my mother and basically turn me back over to her. I was furious! I wanted to scream out, it's not fair! Where do I belong? Where do I fit? Where is my place? This was my loud and clear shout that wherever my fit was it definitely wasn't here and this was one road God threw up roadblocks for me.

At the time I didn't see it that way and I didn't take my friend's warning about my mother. True to his word and almost like a command being carried out by the "King of Teens" my mother was called and I had to go home. I won't go into the gruesome details of the horror of my mother's screeching tires into the apartment complex I was hiding. Needless to say, the time to return to the boundaries set for me had come. Boundaries, whether we like them or not, are there for a reason. Other people play a part in establishing those boundaries and ultimately provide a safe place for us to progress toward our purpose in God.

If you have ever attempted to put a puzzle together, you would know that you face all the pieces upward; examine them and look for the edges. It is these pieces, the pieces with an edge that establish the boundary of the puzzle. The boundary is what gives the Master puzzler a place to start working the vision from. It's the true starting point from which the final work begins to take shape. A puzzle must have a boundary to work from. This is also true in the purposes God has planned for us. He will begin to piece together the vision He has for your life by first establishing where the edge is located and how large the parameter of that vision is. The parameter is determined by how many of those edge pieces are located and eventually connected together.

Think about this. Jesus had his edge pieces in the disciples. Those pieces began to establish the boundaries of His vision for the church. The edge is described by definition "as a place or part farthest away from the center of something." So from that definition, we know the edge is not the heart of the vision or the center of focus. It is however how we get started in that direction.

In our society a person described as being "edgy" is typically someone who is innovative, living life with intensity, excitement, full of new ideas and willing to take risks! These people are often called unique or "outside the box" kind of people. This was not only exciting for me to understand, but encouraging. There is room in God's vision for people with an edge! Those are the people some would call creative, trendsetters or influential to those around them, self-starters and highly motivated.

The vision typically starts with people such as this because they have the measure of faith with the potential for expansion. Have you ever noticed that when a church or business is just starting that it usually begins with people that have the characteristics I just described? The people willing to set the trend and influence others to take part in the vision are those setting the boundaries. Out of all the pieces to a puzzle the edge pieces are the ones who don't have as many opportunities to connect. They have to be willing in some cases to stand with little support around them. That edge is always facing away from the center of the vision. That edge is setting the boundary so the vision can take place. This isn't always the most popular place to be, but without it the vision would operate in chaos. I serve a BIG God who dreams BIG dreams and has BIG plans for my life as well as yours. He does not operate in chaos and he calls those Christians with an edge to set the boundaries. These groups of people help to set boundaries based on their measure of faith which we have already determined is unique and outside the box. We each have been given a measure of faith however, people with an edge caught onto the part of the scripture that our faith has the ability to increase. Those who believe in this ability to increase our measure of faith are typically the ones testing that theory and believing God to do exceedingly and abundant things! It only makes sense to establish God's vision with the ones who are willing to boldly believe in the great things God has planned. Don't misunderstand me and think that all the other pieces are not just as important, but I want you to understand each piece has a place and that place is important to the overall picture and vision of God for the purpose of your life and the church.

Do you remember the story of Elisha and the widow found in 2 Kings chapter 4 of the Bible? God used this story to show me what edgy people look like. When you look back at the story, the widow explained to Elisha that her husband, who had now passed away, was a prior follower of the prophet Elisha. Edgy people know how to find the eccentric men and women of God! The widow's husband recognized the measure of faith in Elisha and witnessed the things God could do within that kind of parameter. The widow must have recognized too because she wasn't afraid to listen to the instruction of Elisha when he came to help her no matter how "edgy" or outside the box it may have sounded. After the widow's husband had passed, we come to the part of the story where Elisha is helping the widow clear her husband's old debt. If you have never read this story, I encourage you to go there now.

2 Kings 4:1-5

*"The wife of a man from the company of the
prophets cried out to Elisha, "Your servant my
husband is dead, and you know that he revered the
Lord. But now his creditor is coming to take my two
boys as his slaves. 2: Elisha replied to her, "How can
I help you? Tell me, what do you have in your
house?" "Your servant has nothing there at all, "she
said, "except a small jar of olive oil." 3: Elisha said,
"Go around and ask all your neighbors for empty
jars. Don't ask for just a few. 4: Then go inside and
shut the door behind you and your sons. Pour oil into
the jars, and as each is filled, put it to one side." 5:
She left him and shut the door behind her and her
sons. They brought the jars to her and she kept
pouring."*

Elisha asked the widow what she had as far as
resources and the widow replied that she had one
bottle of oil. The widow had one other resource as well.
She had lived with a man (her husband) who
demonstrated before her how not to trust in just her
abilities alone but to take a risk on following God. It is
said often in the church that first you must do-- then
watch what God will do.

It says in the Word that this husband was a follower
of Elisha therefore he had already began the process of
expanding the territory or parameter of the life he
wanted for himself and his family. Let's get to the next

part of the story. When the woman declared to Elisha what resources she had, Elisha did not stop there with just a question, he immediately put her faith to action by telling her to go and collect empty jars from her neighbors. The widow by acting on faith now has something to measure her faith by and this sets the tone for my point in this illustration. It is in the ability of the widow to act on the Word of God according to her measure of faith that sets the boundary in which God will operate. Once the widow had collected the jars from her neighbors, the rest of the story goes that what oil she had, began to multiply as she filled the jars and the oil continued to fill all the jars until there were no more jars to be filled.

God used this story to show me what edgy people look like and how important they are to the body of Christ. I don't mean the nervous and unsure kind of edgy. I'm talking about those people with ideas, thoughts, and courage-- not afraid to go when God says go. They are not afraid to ask of people what God tells them to ask. This illustration shows us that as the widow filled the jars, the oil did not run out until the widow ran out of jars and remember I mentioned earlier this act alone was measuring the widow's faith.

God does not limit our vision and purpose in life. The boundaries for our purpose in the body of Christ are set by our own ability to think beyond what is possible by our selves individually versus what is possible with God. This works in two ways. It works for us as individuals when we are setting boundaries for our families, our careers or personal goals in life. It also works in the body of Christ as a whole when God is searching the earth for those people who will believe in His vision and set the boundary from which He can begin to work through us collectively to accomplish His will. With that in mind, we are primarily focusing on the later of the two when speaking of boundaries in this book. We are all given a measure of faith.

Romans 12: 3 NIV
"For by the grace given me I say to every one of you: Do not think of yourself more highly than you ought, but rather think of yourself with sober judgment, in accordance with the measure of faith God has given you."

It is this measure that determines what we will accomplish in our lives and in the body of Christ as a whole. Some Christians have "edgy" measures of faith that allow them to believe for the innovative, exciting and permissible things of God. When you gather them all together they create the boundary for the vision God wants to happen for His church body. Thank God for edgy people willing to think outside the box and believe in the bigger picture!

In the story of the widow, Elisha did not ask the woman to create more jars. Christians can get very busy working on the wrong things for God. When this happens we have left the plans, purposes and visions of God. This is why boundaries are important. They show us where to focus our efforts so the vision continues to progress. Without a boundary or parameter, the vision is left unprotected. The vision gets disturbed when any and everyone are allowed to break through the boundary of the vision. It is also important to note that you can't protect the vision alone. You and you alone cannot be the boundary of the vision God has for your life. It will take connecting with others.

Elisha then instructed the widow to go to her neighbors and collect more jars. It is no coincidence that God will not only use what we have but often times what we have has to be used in conjunction with what others have. For the purpose of this book, Elisha might as well have asked the widow to go to her neighbors and connect rather than collect. It is this process of connecting that we begin to find ourselves increasing our measure of faith in areas we may have never imagined. It is through others that God works with us and through us. Get connected with some other people who will believe for the permissible, innovative and exciting things of God for your life and the Church. The boundaries set by your local church are usually determined by the belief system of the leaders of the Church and how much of God's vision for that house they can believe in. Those individuals begin to form the "edgy" boundary for that local church body.

One definition of the word boundary is described as "a parameter, measurable factor that defines a system with set conditions of operation." Some would say the boundary is limiting, but I believe in a God that is limitless! Connect with the wisdom of God in this area of your life. Without boundaries or limits, identities become blurred in the body of Christ and life in general. We have to believe that God can use us where we are and for who we are. My piece of the puzzle may be different from yours, but each piece is vital to the inner workings of God's vision because He created us with his vision in mind. Remember, we said that we were not created after the vision. We were thought of as an original part of the vision. I've witnessed personally how groups of people begin something without ever setting up specific conditions for how their ministry, family, career goals, personal life, etc., will operate. This is not safe because the enemy can catch us off guard more quickly this way. Boundaries affect both what is coming in and what is going out of our territory in Christ. Think about that for a moment. If you don't allow God to set boundaries in all areas of your life, there is a lack of control over what is being allowed in and out of your life in that area. Without proper boundaries, it is difficult for God to protect your marriage or bless your marriage for example. This is also true with the vision God has for your career or other dreams and goals for yourself. Imagine God trying to bless you, but without boundaries the enemy gets in and steals your blessings. This will often take cooperation and connection to others God has sent for the very purpose of protecting and blessing the vision for that area of your life. Boundaries have to be established and early on in the vision. So many of us want to connect with others to get our blessings first! THEN we want to go back and figure out ways to protect what we have after it manifests. This is out of order, because while you are going BACK to establish a boundary your blessing is left unattended. It is left unprotected. So many Christians have been on this hamster wheel for years. We haven't built our faith enough to trust others God has sent our way to establish boundaries for our life. This comes down to not only trusting others God has sent to us, but ultimately it comes down to trusting God. We discussed at the beginning of this book regarding heart issues and that trust is key. You have to trust God has your best interest at heart. He establishes boundaries to protect the vision He has for us which ultimately guides us to our purpose in Christ Jesus. Don't be afraid to trust. You should be afraid NOT to. Trust and obey, for there is no better way.

Recently, the pastor of the church I attend taught on the prayer of Jabez. This was perfect timing in my life because I had been feeling as if my boundaries were to small for the visions I had been viewing for my life. I was then and still do have dreams that continue to stretch my faith on a daily basis. In order for those dreams to come to pass, I had to re-examine my boundaries. This ultimately pushed me to examine my trust in God. Through that teaching on the prayer of Jabez, I discovered how to increase my boundaries for the visions God was giving to me. I had to first trust God and eventually trust others in order for my territory to expand. This began a connecting domino effect with the people in my life and in other areas of my circle of influence. Connections that had been there all along began to come into place and form boundaries for the vision God was giving me. I am speaking currently of individual vision however God has an overall vision for the Church and the process works the same way.

Are you figuring out that each of our individual purposes ARE the collective vision for the Church? That's another book, but just focus on your piece of the puzzle in the general purposes God has for your life right now. Allow God to establish boundaries. Don't be afraid to connect to others by ultimately trusting the God who gives you purpose and vision in the first place. You can't protect and serve at the same time. We have heard that said of men and women in service positions such as the police and fire department. They "protect and serve" and this is true, but they don't do these things at the same time. What do I mean? To truly protect is to stand guard, be on the look out. When danger is spotted it is then time to serve. It does not service me if my house is on fire and the fire fighters stand guard while it burns to the ground. We have to accept the place we are at the appropriate times during our journey. Know your place and how it functions. Stop trying to be something you are not! If you are an "edgy" piece, stand your ground, protect as God leads you and serve when it is time. There is order to God's visions and purposes for our lives.

You might be asking yourself, what is my piece of the puzzle. It may not be that you are that "edgy" piece we have been speaking of. That is okay! We are not finished with the puzzle yet! Keep reading! There is a place for each of us.

I began to find my purpose and place in God's vision when I had done some of these things we have been speaking of. After my spiritual heart surgery, I was ready to find my place and get actively moving into the things God had for me. The next step was simple. You have not because you ask not.

James 4:2-3 NIV
"You desire but do not have, so you kill. You covet but you cannot get what you want, so you quarrel and fight. You do not have because you do not ask God. 3:When you ask, you do not receive, because you ask with wrong motives, that you may spend what you get on your pleasures."

I had begun to ask God to expand my territory, my parameters of belief, my boundaries in Christ Jesus and that my motives would be in the right place. Immediately after you ask God for something, don't forget to establish boundaries to protect your answer from the enemy. Understand that even if you are not that "edgy" piece of the puzzle you will need to connect to some "edgy" people to assist you in establishing a boundary for the vision God has given you. These people will help you to take the next steps in fulfilling your purpose. This step was truly amazing for me as I began to find there were others who believed in who I am as a Christian and YES they were willing to connect with me and believe with me in fulfilling my purpose in the body of Christ. These people can see what is coming in and what is going out of your vision. Trust God! These pieces to the puzzle of your purpose help protect the inner workings of what God is doing in your life. The connecting power of these pieces, establish the unlimited ability of God to work according to the measure of faith your boundary pieces are built from. Again, this same principle works for us as individuals as well as the over all church.

Connection is powerful! If we do it the right way and in the right order you will find out who you are in Christ and the part you play in the vision. Now if you are not that edgy piece of the puzzle, don't forget what was explained earlier that each piece is important and absolutely plays a part in the vision, pre-planned and pre-destined by God. Don't give up before we establish where you fit. Without these "edge" pieces, it would be difficult to complete the puzzle. God will seek out the "edge" pieces first in order to contain the vision. It is a safe place to start any vision God has for your life. It will take cooperation from these "edgy" believers to protect and serve the vision. Connecting through relationships will create the boundary or parameter in which God sets the conditions for us to progress the vision and operate safely.

1 Corinthians 14:33 NIV
"For God is not a God of disorder but of peace-as in all the congregations of the Lord's people."

This connecting process keeps the vision of God in a forward progressively moving order.

Chapter Four

SORTING

"I choose to make the most of my life and not spend the majority of my time on the small things I cannot change."
Tasha Hart

As you see by my stories from childhood to adulthood, I was rebellious. Anything that made me uncomfortable or out of sorts made me rebel against the system whether it is against God or the world. Things we don't understand or things that make us uncomfortable can prompt us to run away. This reaction is not always what God wants from us. Finding our fit and purpose in God will require us to stand in some uncomfortable situations and allow Him to sort it all out. Often times it is through this sorting process that we get one step closer to where we need to be in fulfilling our purpose. How we react to the sorting process is a clear demonstration of how much we trust the God we serve. I had to learn to trust God with my whole heart and not just with my mind.

Early on in childhood you begin to subtly learn some of those basic rules that eventually come up in your adult life. The sorting process was no different. Whenever it was time to play hide-n-go seek the sorting process began. Who will go first ini- mini-miny-moe and soforth. This made the selection and sorting process pretty simple. As I got older, it was heartbreaking to find that things didn't quite work the same way. Wouldn't it be nice during raise time to just put your foot in the circle and let the selection sort itself out? I didn't have issues with this process when I was younger because I didn't experience the heartbreak of being left out. What do I mean? When I was younger and we played those childhood games or a few back yard rounds of base ball the sorting process was simple. You were always selected and you didn't care so much what you were selected for, as long as you got to play and be a part of the game. How this mindset changes over time. Eventually, positioning becomes important and the sorting process more serious and you are not guaranteed a position in the game at all. As this becomes more and more the norm, you find yourself doing things like competing. If you don't experience the right results you can become leery of this sorting process all together. You begin to doubt your "worthiness" or worse you become disillusioned with everyone around you and figure why bother.

I caution you as you read this chapter to ignore the urge and habit of feeling either of those ways. Forget what your childhood and past have told you about this sorting process. Don't allow prior experiences with this process to stop you from receiving all this chapter has to offer. I want you to know that God has a sorting process and His ways are higher than our ways. His thoughts are higher than our thoughts. This time, the sorting process will be different and this time, you don't have to worry yourself with competing for a position, doubting your capabilities or with the tireless urge to gain the acceptance of others. This time, you will understand why this process will help you and not harm you. You have already been chosen!

We have talked about getting out of the box explaining the importance of leaving our comfort zone so God can begin to move us into His vision for our lives. Once we have left our comfort zone, it is important to not sit still. We are going to take a closer look at fitting into God's vision. It's not easy to examine yourself and view yourself the way God views you.

Psalm 139: 14 NIV
"I praise you because I am fearfully and wonderfully made; your works are wonderful, I know that full well."

This verse of scripture says we are fearfully and wonderfully made. One definition for fearfully says it means dauntless which means incapable of being intimidated or discouraged, another definition says bold". Looking back at Psalm 139:14, I can see that I am made bold incapable of being intimidated or discouraged.

I may "feel" these things but I don't have to let them dictate my actions. This verse in scripture ends with a reminder that we are wonderfully made. Examining the definition of the word wonderfully, we find that it means inspiring delight, pleasure, extremely good, marvelous and the Word says this is how we were created. I'm spending time here because you have to believe what the Word says about you before you will believe what the Word has for you. A person who is fearfully and wonderfully made will find this sorting and connecting process just another step in fitting into the purpose God has created for you.

What is it about you that will allow you to have an advantage for the Kingdom, that allows you to connect, that allows you to fit where God has envisioned you? Looking at your list, you may begin to find clues to this question. During this next stage you will find yourself being sorted by God into small groups. When a master puzzler gets to this stage of the puzzle they sort the pieces into piles based on color or similarities determined by the design of the puzzle, itself. If we look at this step in a spiritual sense, you will find that God, the Master puzzle solver, does the same thing. He will begin to sort us out into smaller groups according to similarities determined by His great design and ultimate vision. The Master moves us around a little bit in groups where we will eventually connect to others. The question is, are you willing to be moved by God?

Looking back on my high school years, it was a difficult time for me. I have always been the type of person who thrived on blending in and being a "part" of the group. No one likes the feeling of being left out! I also was the class clown, which lent itself to fitting into certain areas of the high school crowd. It is funny how laughter is universal. I did notice however that the "in" crowd was harder to penetrate. They didn't walk like I walked. They didn't talk like I talked, but they seemed to be having the time of their young lives! I purposely took classes that put me in the unpopular groups so to speak, so that I could excel without the pressure of fitting into the popular groups. That experience among others, taught me the value of respecting all types of people and appreciating God's creations. I remember a particular student in one of those "unpopular" classes. Thinking of his high school experience reminded me how sometimes as Christians we allow others around us to dictate how we move in the body of Christ. This student was awkward and shy most of the time. He was very plain and thin. He did have a good sense of humor and so I would laugh with him sometimes. We never became good friends. I tried to make it a point to acknowledge him because he was severely picked on in high school. He was teased and pushed around often. Various people (myself included) would stick up for him from time-to-time, but all through high school this was his lot. I remember when it was close to our senior year that this student had changed and not for the better. It seemed that the three plus years of torment had taken its toll on this student and he became mean. He would even poke back at me and the other students, who once would stick up for him. He had decided that instead of finding where he did fit in and accepting those willing to accept him that he would reject the entire process of connecting all together! This is a lonely place of bitterness and resentment that as it grows, limits the possibility of viewing God's intentions for your life. I'm writing this book because I sincerely believe God wants more from us at this time and this hour of His vision. He wants us to get in where we fit in! He wants you to be open to this stage of being sorted, arranged, MOVED by God.

In the story about the bullied and then sullen student I went to high school with, I wanted to show the importance of connecting to others in these small groups settings. God will begin to sort you into areas that require you to connect with others. You may not always like the people God has arranged you to connect with, but His ways are not our ways. His vision goes beyond our limited vision. He can see the beginning and the end. We have to connect with those who will not only encourage us but also challenge our growth in the body of Christ. This part of the connecting process requires faith on our part. There is that familiar word again. Faith. Faith! Faith! I know it is a common word but it is such an uncommon thing and as Christians we are called to be uncommon among the world's standards. The world is telling us that being sorted is the same as separation. This is not true! The world is blurring the lines or sorting and calling it separation and discrimination.

According to Webster's New World Dictionary for Young Readers "to sort means to arrange into different sets according to common distinctions among two or more things". This is part of God's creation. He sorted us by plant, animal, man, resources, etc. Everywhere in life that we look, there is this sorting that takes place. Sorting involves grouping together two or more things with common distinctions. The sands at the bottom of the ocean do not question the body of water that flows over it. They are sorted apart, but work together.

This is not the same as separation or discrimination that categorizes people specifically based on race, age or sex in order to provide unjust or prejudicial treatment. God sorts us to enhance our differences and allow us to utilize those for the building of the body of Christ. Discrimination takes us away from the connecting process by separating us from the possible people God may use to propel us farther. We do not want to discriminate, but we do want to participate in this sorting process having faith that God will bring us together to work with His other children that have distinct talents, ideas and resources that compliment one another. This is opposite of what the world says. You have to be sorted--not separated. There are distinctions between us from our hair color to gender, talents and thought processes. We have distinctions for a reason and these distinctions help us to find our fit. By faith we utilize our distinct differences to put our faith to work. Faith calls us to action! In James the second chapter, it begins to break down this idea of faith.

James 2:14 NIV
"What good is it, my brothers and sisters, if someone claims to have faith but has no deeds? Can such faith save them?"

James 2:14 asks us what is the purpose of having faith if we don't prove it by our actions? Sometimes the action step is not really action on our part at all. Sometimes the action required by us is plain obedience. You see this in the body of Christ within small groups. We are sorted out into smaller groups to receive instruction that allows the Teacher (Holy Spirit) to work closer, answering our questions and concerns, allowing us to connect through obedience and faith. Are you willing to say to God, where you go, I go, what you say, I will do, who you say to connect with, I will connect with? This process of connecting to those God has surrounded us with is for us to put our faith into action. It is our chance to show God our obedience in cooperation with His vision and His will for our lives. God meets our needs, physically, emotionally and spiritually through our day-to-day connections to the people He places in our lives. It may not always be a smooth connection, however even the rough connections have a way of smoothing us out in areas we had no idea needed some work. It is this day-to-day obedience that brings us closer to seeing God's vision for our lives.

I pray for those reading these words right now to begin to seek obedience quicker in the areas of life God has sorted you to. Look at every person in your life as a potential connection to the vision of God for your life. Practice daily obedience in the areas that you are weakest. If patience is an issue, spend more time with that person at work that you don't always have the greatest patience with. Rely on the Word of God to sustain you through these practices. If you are struggling in an area of connecting with others, get in the Word and practice.

Remind yourself that it is not about you but it is about the God who sent His Son for you and I to have life more abundantly. That abundant life comes through day-to-day interaction and connecting with that person who knows another person who knows the right person to get you one piece closer to God's vision and purpose for your life. Looking at James 2:17, we can see that it's not enough to just have faith.

James 2:17 NIV
"In the same way, faith by itself, if it is not accompanied by action, is dead."

You have to prove yourself faithful by your actions. This is different from just plain works. Works are what I want to do to prove myself faithful but obedience is simply doing the work God wants me to do to show myself faithful and committed to His plan and His vision. Are you willing to be moved by God? Are you willing to have faith that moves beyond what you want to do? Have you decided to get into the Word of God and simply be obedient on a day-to-day basis? Have you decided to be committed to the connections God has placed around you for not only your growth, but the growth of His body in Jesus Christ? Matthew 7:24 reminds us that your obedience is what God requires of you.

Matthew 7:24 NIV
"Therefore everyone who hears these words of mine and puts them into practice is like a wise man who built his house on the rock."

Be a part of what God is doing. Find your purpose! Be willing to connect with those around you. Enjoy the sorting process because it is through this process that you begin to practice obedience and build your faith in who God created you to be!

The decision to fit into the vision of God is truly an act of deciding to move beyond your intentions to impact. You have to focus on the why of your heart and allow it to guide your behavior. Intentions are invisible to people, but clear to God. Intentions are defined in Webster's New World Dictionary for Young Readers as anything planned or purposed. The definition of intent is having the mind or attention fixed; concentrating, firmly directed.

The blood of Jesus Christ has a planned purpose, firmly directed to areas of the body concentrating on what it was sent to do. How do we know if the intentions of the blood are fulfilling the planned purpose? We look at the behavior of the body to see how it was impacted. Let's piece all of this together. If the spiritual heart can be defined as our intentions we have to move beyond "good" intentions and firmly concentrate on what we were created to do, allowing the life-blood of Jesus Christ to flow from us to other connecting parts of the body. You will know you have moved beyond "good" intentions to a fitted and fixed purpose when you can look at the reaction of the Body of Christ and see the "impact"! I challenge you today to do more than aimlessly find a place to fit into the body of Christ. No! Don't do that! Examine the intentions of your heart, the why behind your decisions, the concentrated purpose of your plans and then choose to fit in. Ask God to show you where you will have the most impact, based on your unique design. You were fearfully and wonderfully made, remember? We all play a part in this interconnecting process.

Chapter Five

CONNECTING

"I've always had big dreams and I'm just now realizing that it was the people in my dreams that made them so big. You can't achieve a big dream alone."

Tasha Hart

Why is connection so important? What is the purpose behind connection? I believe connection is just another way of describing family and family is very important to God. Family has a purpose and God Himself desired a family. Enough said right? It is within this family you will find your purpose. Ephesians 2:18-19 gives us some insight as to why connection is important.

Ephesians 2: 18-19
"For through him we both have access to the Father by one Spirit. 19, consequently, you are no longer foreigners and aliens, but fellow citizens with God's people and members of God's household."

In the King James Version, this verse describes our citizenship with God's people as being members of His family. This verse reminds us that we each as believers are now a part. We are not on the outside looking in but we have inside access. Connection provides us with family and access to all that family has to offer. There is support and safety within a family. I know this is true even more so with the family of God because of the example of a family on earth. My brothers are very protective of my sisters and I. There is something about being blood-related that causes you to protect one another! You don't talk about my mama, you don't threaten my sisters and you don't try to harm my brothers unless you want to address the entire family! This is how my earthly family operates and I believe the family of God operates in a similar way. There is strength in numbers and this is why the enemy works tirelessly to destroy connections or prevent us from connecting all together.

In the body of Christ, my position in the family was bought with a price. Ephesians 2:13 explains:

> *"But now in Christ Jesus you who once were far away have been brought near through the blood of Christ."*

Reading this verse, I am reminded how many times I did not allow myself to connect with the family of God, my family. I felt as if I didn't belong; why would Christ accept me? I had to look closer at this and realize my place was bought with the blood of the Lord! How many of us make excuses why we won't take up our blessings and carry on with thanksgiving? Some of us would even say we are being humble when we turn down the gifts of God. It's time to stop walking away from our place in the Family of God! How many of us would turn down free tickets to see our favorite music artist or actor/actress with an invite to stay over night as a guest? Seriously? I would be excited! Thrilled for the once in a lifetime opportunity! Yet, every day I'm invited to do just that with the King of Kings! Some Christians make this mistake over and over again by turning down a gift that has already been bought with such a high price. We don't honor the Father by turning down the invitation! It is not an act of humility to put our lives aside and allow everyone else in the world to have a say in how we live our lives except the one that created us.

Having a chameleon personality, I didn't have a problem blending into any environment I was subjected to. I actually became an expert at it. However blending in is not the same as truly connecting. Awhile back I would have told you that this chameleon personality of mine was a weakness. This is what the enemy (our adversary the devil) would have liked me to believe. Since writing this book, I have come to an understanding about weaknesses. They are usually not weaknesses at all, they are usually our strengths but misguided. What do I mean? My ability to blend can be a weakness if I use that ability to hide from those around me and not engage them for the glory of God! However, if I use my ability to blend and make those around me feel comfortable, I have an open door to speak into the lives of those that may not have listened to what I had to say otherwise. I've actually found this to be one of my better strengths that the enemy had convinced me was a weakness for years. I was told that I was a hypocrite because I would speak to those that some considered backbiters or mean. How could I speak and interact with the very same people that did not like me? In some cases it didn't have to do with me at all. Some people are just not comfortable around other people and that is where God made me capable. I could fit in with the unwelcomed, misunderstood, old, young, mean, nice, black, white, Chinese or Spanish and so forth. I looked for the common thread and became whatever made that person feel connected. Looking back on this kind of interaction, made me realize with a passion how effective and important connection was and still is. I'm not saying you have to be like me and just connect with everyone but I am saying there is someone you are created to connect with and it is important to the body of Christ that you find out who that person or persons are in your life.

After my spiritual heart surgery, I began to see how I had missed so many opportunities in my life to truly connect with those God had sent in my path. I can't blame myself for what I didn't know then. There comes a point in your life when you have to accept that you have and will make mistakes. It is key that you don't dwell on those mistakes but continue to learn from them. That is what this is, a learning process in which you take what you missed before and apply it to where you are now. You can't allow the hurts of your past to keep you puzzled and confused.

This is another trick of the enemy to keep you from connecting. When you are hurt and broken it makes this connecting process seem almost impossible. I am grateful for my Lord and Savior who never gives up on us, or our destiny in Him. There were times in my life that influenced my difficulty with connecting with others. I had been seeking for most of my life to fit in for one reason or another. I was collecting answers to my queries the same as some women collect shoes. You have a certain pair for a certain occasion and you have that pair you ONLY wear with that specific outfit you bought it to match with. This was how my life was developing. I found that I had certain answers I had collected that fit during certain occasions. Again the enemy had fooled me into thinking my ability to blend was for the purpose of hiding and only living life to please others. If I blended in and didn't cause a commotion, people liked me and at the same time forgot about me. I was okay with that as long as I didn't upset people and get out of line or cause trouble. Or so, I thought. I just wanted to blend in. For example, I had the best ways to ace an interview and give the interviewer what they had been waiting to hear five people before you! I knew how to blend, but after the correct answers were given at the best opportune times I would still be lacking in true connection. Was I invited to prom? Yes, but I didn't go because I didn't really know the guy that asked me. Was I invited to football games under Friday night-lights? Yes, but I would get lost in translation because I wasn't at the last game. Was I invited to lunches, brunches and dinners with co-workers and friends? Yes, but in a room full of laughter, I just didn't seem to get the jokes. Where was the true connection? Moving around a lot during my childhood wasn't to blame. It didn't help equip me for the time-consuming task of true connection.

I began to view people as simply that, people. Like chess pieces in the game of life, you move them around strategically or you get attacked from the opposite side and removed from the game all together. I joined the chess club in high school to see if maybe, just maybe, I'd fit in with the chess "geeks". I learned how to play the game but I still didn't find my fit! In less than four moves, I was out of the "club" and back in the game of life. I ran track but I wasn't the fastest. At a track meet once, I was asked by my coach to run a long distance competition. I was a sprinter. I didn't think about that fact when my coach asked me to fill in for one of our long distance runners that I couldn't be there for this particular meet. I wanted to please the coach. I figured this was my opportunity to show I was a team player and I belonged. I will never forget taking off around the track full speed thinking to myself how easy this was. I had overlapped the other runners by at least two maybe three laps. Little did I know long distance runners pace themselves so not to tire out too quickly. I came in last place. Embarrassed about my quick start and extremely slow finish, I stopped running track and decided to try out for softball. That is another list of embarrassing stories but there is something about being a Christian and saved at an early age that almost forces you forward.

With all the frustrations of life and misunderstandings, my lack of connections and true connection with people only pushed me to keep searching. That is the amazing thing about God, if you keep seeking Him, He won't disappoint you. In fact, you will connect to the Father's heart and run right smack dab into the middle of your purpose. You can't allow the enemy to isolate you from the Father's heart. He loves you. He loves us so much He created this universe for us to explore, experience and connect. Engage it with all you are and all you were created to be!

I was teased a lot when I was younger. Surprise, surprise! I was too light to be accepted by my own race and I was too dark to be accepted by the other so I found myself both the black and the white sheep all at the same time. This may have been enough to push some people over the edge and for me it did but not necessarily in a bad way. I can't explain this paradox of being able to fit in at times and at others being a complete outsider. Again, I just have to say it has worked for me in areas when God wanted to use me to connect with someone. Other times when I just wanted to be accepted it didn't always work.

We all have that tenacity inside us. During certain times in our lives this one thing about us is what keeps us hoping in our future! It's what makes us unique or it might be one of many things, the key is to accept who you are and not wait for others to follow suit. You need room for this acceptance and growth process to take place. For me it was that little white house on the corner in that small town in Indiana that gave me room to grow in areas that have set the course for my life. My grandfather never pressured me to do anything except be myself! In those times when I felt like the black or white sheep, disconnected from true love and acceptance, I could excel in the area of insight and imagination. When no one was accepting me, God used those times in my life to accept others. It's hard to focus on what you don't have when you are focused on other people.

Again to list all the people I've had the privilege of meeting and learning from would take a book all by itself! I will mention a few including the time I spent with various woman of a particular age, some of whom I've mentioned already. I say these women were of a particular age but these women were far from that in personality and character. Many of these women lived near the homes I stayed in growing up, whose children, some close to my age or older, lived far away and only visited a couple times a year. Visiting with them gave them an outlet to share their stories of child rearing and pass down some words of wisdom they just knew I would eventually need. True to their insight some of that wisdom continues to be useful in my life and I'm forever grateful.

Connection can happen anywhere and at any given time if you are open to it like the times I used to volunteer at a restoration home. I was in high school and lived in Maryland at the time. I'm mentioning these stories because I want you to just get a glimpse of how some situations in your life may appear to be one way to you but in actuality they could be connection points along the way that bring you closer to your destiny. Some connections are brief and others will help you access what not to do in the future. It all plays a part in shaping who you are. At the restoration home, I had met and spent time with one of the original Rockettes. She was stuck in her past but it was beautiful to watch. She still loved to sing and dance and would perform regularly for the residents. I would watch as God showed me the lives and stories of those around me who ultimately in some way, could identify with what I was feeling. Disconnected. There had to be a reason God wanted me to see these people through His eyes.

There was the nerd in school no one truly spoke to and I could see he was a kid that still needed to be seen, so I made it a point to find out what types of things he liked and strike up conversations. We talked about chemistry and his enjoyment as a volunteer fire fighter. I didn't have a clue what all that meant but I think it took his mind off the reality of being left out at times.

One of my favorite teachers LOVED "The Wizard of Oz" and had a collection out of this world. That just so happens to still be one of my all-time favorite movies because that teacher would allow me to stay after school and admire her collection of memorabilia. She explained to me the history of the characters and all kinds of interesting facts about how the movie was made. It was like watching an adult kid and I got to share in her excitement. It was a connecting point and I don't even know if she realized it at the time. All I can say is that I still remember her face as she talked about one of the favorite things in her life and I felt special that she shared that with me.

My world has been filled with countless memories and experiences. I've had the honor and privilege of sharing and it all led me to believe that God wanted these moments for Himself. Connection is important because we as children of God are important. Now is the time to help people learn what true connection is all about. Now is the time to explain the heart of the Father and share with others that even if it's brief, even if it's not what you think or how you thought it should be, connection, happens around us, through us and to us daily because the Father wants to share in those moments that make you special to Him. He wants to be the Father of your life and have His family close to Him. As I've gotten older I've also gotten a stronger sense of why God wanted me to see these people. He loves them, as much as He loves you and I! He wanted me to see them and how different they were and that it didn't make a difference to Him. It didn't matter if they were old, young, white, black, smart or what church they went to or what kind of childhood they had. He loved them and by loving these people and appreciating their stories, I began loving them too! That was the connection God wanted me to make! It was a connection between God and His people and you can be connected, too. You just have to see it the way God views it and know why your connection is so important to the rest of us. You will realize why my connection is so important to you!

People with an edge have been identified and connected to create our boundary. Individual remaining pieces to the puzzle have been sorted into groups according to their design, similarities and abilities. It is now time to address each group in sections. It is amazing to me how people stop progressing forward after the last action or instruction given. God may instruct an individual to find a church home and for weeks they search out the place that seems to fit for them. Once they discover the place God wants them to be, often times they stop right there. They immediately take the position of spectator rather than a continued player in the game. I've heard it explained by my pastor on many occasions how often new-comers join the church and then immediately "take their seat". They stop participating in the process of seeking what God has next and expect others around them to take it from there. The "I'm here" mentality, now what are you going to do to help me, is not the kind of attitude that will get that person connected to their purpose! We have to move forward with the connecting process if we want to continue getting closer to the heartbeat of the Father. This will require more than just showing up. I've known families who have shown up for each other for years but never truly interacted with one another. There are families today that as soon as the work day is over they go home and find more busy work to do that keeps them separated from their loved ones. Children are in their room more than they are with their family. Where is the connection? It doesn't always have to be a special holiday that brings us together. Everyday with Jesus is a holiday! Every morning is a new day of connection waiting to happen. You have to get into a good church and hear the Word! Yes! Then continue forward and don't just hear the Word. Put some action behind what you're hearing!

James 1:22 NIV
"Do not merely listen to the word, and so deceive yourselves. Do what it says."

Don't just hear! Do! That is what connection requires. If someone opened the box, took out all the puzzle pieces but never began the connection process the previous work would be in vain. Don't stop connection before the vision is complete. We can't be satisfied being a hearer of the Word. To hear only is a set up for deception. They are typically the ones who show up faithfully and believe that by observing alone they can give wise counsel and correction to others, however they have never taken action to walk out what they are saying. There isn't substantial evidence in their lives to show us they live out and connect with the Word they are preaching. This is sad because they know the truth; but do they truly believe it! Why would I even open the box if I didn't believe the pieces would all fit together and the puzzle could be completed? Why waste my time? Why waste yours? I urge you to not stop now but continue on and do something with the truth you have been entrusted with. Do something with His Word. Make connections that touch the Father's heart.

Lets look at our attitudes. Attitudes can direct our attention toward or away from connection. Throughout these chapters we have been discussing the similarities between piecing together a physical puzzle with the realities of piecing together our purposes in the body of

Christ. One of the major things to remember is that this takes some mental strength to accomplish. Remember when you are piecing a puzzle together, you are using intellect to solve a problem. I call this the "puzzling mentality." It is the steps an individual takes to get beyond an issue to actually solving a problem. This type of mentality requires a person to ponder on possibilities, discover what resources are available, reasoning logistics and applying action until something works. This is repeated over and over again, piece-by-piece, section-by-section until the vision is complete. The good news is that God has given us all the pieces necessary to complete the vision! We don't have to concern ourselves that we will work hard on the vision God has for us only to discover there is a piece missing and the vision will be incomplete. He will and has provided all you need for the vision ahead of you! That is the difference between a "puzzling" mentality and a "puzzled" mentality. Be careful how you examine the two because they can seem very much the same on casual glance. A person with a puzzling mentality focuses on taking risks to work toward a solution. A person who is puzzled is so focused on the risks they stay stagnant in a state of constant confusion. A puzzled person is not an effective person because they are not willing to be moved, worked or used in the solution process. A puzzled person believes that figuring things out is the same as moving in faith. This is not so. Sometimes you may not have things all figured out before you are required to act in faith. That is the reason for faith in the first place-- to move us beyond our own understanding into areas we can only operate with God. It is sad to say but I have witnessed Christians that have left this world still in the puzzled stage of life. They were confused about what it was they were really here to do and because they didn't have things all figured out they stopped moving forward! These people stopped connecting.

It is great to find yourself out of the box and open to the things God has planned however this is not the time to stop and allow confusion to block the connection process. We have to participate in the entire process from beginning to end, taking up responsibility for our role in the vision. We can't join a church, a job, a family, a marriage or any other group without contributing what is expected of us. We won't always know what to expect next but it's okay, make some choices to connect and don't stay puzzled in one place for the rest of your life! Puzzled people sit back and wait for someone to notice them, their talents and/or gifts before offering them as a reasonable service to the body of Christ. A puzzled person has to be asked over and over again to volunteer because they are unsure of themselves and their place. Someone unwilling to go through this working process will usually isolate themselves from the group or the process and make excuses as to why they have not found where they fit. Puzzled people spend more time puzzled than pursuing their purpose.

On the contrary, a puzzling person is someone who is unique, working outside the box to create opportunities to use their gifts. A puzzling person commands attention with Christ's confidence in what they were created to be. A puzzling person strengthens the body of Christ by their ability to solve problems that hinder the vision of God for the Church. Puzzling people are a force unified in one thing, connecting with boldness to achieve the purposes of God. They don't quit! They will turn a piece around several times, testing connections, resolving issues, working each area piece-by-piece to see the vision of God grow. They are committed to uniting for the common good of the body of Christ.

At some point in my life, I have found myself in one thought pattern or the other. The times I found myself in the puzzled thought pattern were some of the loneliest and most confusing times of my life! I would join a church, find "my seat" and keep to myself. I did not put forth much effort to meet others or connect with them and then would go home feeling even more isolated than I did before I went to church! I was that person that in a room full of people I'd feel utterly and completely alone because something or someone had affected the way I felt about connection. This is no excuse because ultimately my connecting with others is about God and not about me. When I make it about me, I open myself up for deception and hurt feelings. When

I make it about Him, I get those rare glimpses into God's plan for His family and it is amazing!

Looking back now I can't even begin to describe the amount of time I wasted creating problems for myself rather than being a problem-solver. I allowed things from my past, my childhood, my failed relationships and other issues to stunt my ability to connect! I remember when I was around twelve or thirteen visiting my aunt for the day while my grandparents were at work. It was summer and this was routine for my siblings and I to visit my aunt and play with my cousins during the day. This day was no exception. Only that day held a life-changing incident that would continue to define other moments in my life from that point forward. I was outside and my older cousin asked me a question I wasn't prepared for. She just casually asked me where my father was. Being that I was twelve and had no reason to think anything otherwise I answered, "He is at work but he is coming to get me after he gets off." She commented back to me, "not that dad, your REAL dad." I almost thought I misunderstood her and decided that was the case and repeated my first answer back to her. My older cousin again replied, "not that dad, your real dad" adding "the light skinned one" to the original comment. I still remember that day like it was yesterday because it froze everything in me that I thought I knew about myself up to that point in my life.

You may be saying that I was too young for that instance to make that big of an impact on my ability to connect with others. I would ask you to speak to any Christian with some time in their walk with God and see how much of an impact their early experiences in the faith has impacted the way they connect to the body of Christ. I remember thinking to myself that my cousin was teasing me since this was common among children and that's what children do. I thought she was just being the older teasing the younger and that this joke would be over soon. It wasn't over and in fact it had only just begun because when my dad had gotten off work he came to pick me up. He could tell I had this puzzled look on my face and there was the first sign of confusion.

I didn't understand why my cousin would ask me such a question so I finally went from puzzled to puzzling when I got determined to get an answer. I turned to my dad while riding in the front seat of his red Escort GT and simply asked the question, ("daddy, are you my real dad")? I almost laughed as I asked the question thinking he was going to confirm that my cousin had been teasing me all along but the look now on his face proved otherwise. He was not laughing with me and in fact he was not looking at me either. He stared out over the dashboard into the traffic and businesses of the streets and without looking away from the road answered, "go ask your mother." I could have exploded into tears but my heart was racing and I was afraid if I cried it would make matters worse and I could possibly go into cardiac arrest at the age of twelve or so. I'll never forget my mother's confirmation of the confusing but final truth that my dad, who by the way I still call dad today, was not my biological father. So many unanswered questions and now the enemy would use this puzzled state to make me lose sight of where I belong for years to come. I had a distorted view on connecting. I now felt like the outsider with no true connection. What had changed? My perception. I still had a dad who loved me and treated me like his own. I had a father who was there for me when it was time to do my homework, played games with me and protected me. I still had a father who loved me but I no longer loved myself because I lost my perception on how I thought I fit into the vision of my family.

This is so true when it comes to how we connect within the areas God has placed us. Our perception of who we are and who we belong to will determine how well we connect to others and how we proceed through life. Each of us fit where we belong for a reason. My biological father did not raise me, but my Father in heaven knew what was best for me and eventually, I changed my perspective. I was blessed to have the father that raised me when some children grew up without a father. It has helped shape me into the person God wants to use to connect with others and bring connection among His people.

If we were meant to be alone, isolated and disconnected one from another God would not care so much about family, marriage, friendships and relationships in general. He puts us into groups that will utilize our spiritual gifts, talents and creative shape to connect His vision among us. If God is not satisfied being alone, neither should we be satisfied with that state of being. There has to be more action on our part than just showing up. There comes a time to start making choices that will determine what part of the vision you will fit into. Previously, we talked about how God will sort you into groups that He has designed for you based on certain criteria. Remaining in the "sorted" stage will not get you to the completed vision that God has for your life. You are not only to show up, you also have to show out! That's what Jesus did. He showed up and then He showed out by connecting with people. Don't get me wrong, we want people to show up but then they must begin to take their place by asking questions and seeking God for the truth.

Allow the group you are in to be your springboard. This is the time to discover your talents, explore your spiritual gifts, practice what you preach, be strengthened in your inner man, ask for help, pray through and then pray with others, connect and continue toward God's purpose. This is how this connecting process works. When putting together a puzzle (and all the pieces are spread out on the surface) it would be a shame to never connect all the pieces. At some point, to see the completed vision there has to be a willingness to be moved, worked, turned around and connected. How silly would it be if after the pieces were sorted into these groups or piles that the pieces were never connected? Some Christians get comfortable in the pile. They don't mind being hidden within the group. They don't mind appearing to be connected when they are simply showing up. I have seen in some circles and small groups where people will show up for years and never truly connect. People like this won't take risks, invest action with their time, and see what else God wants to do with their gifts, talents and abilities. It's about people, so if people make you uncomfortable, that is the pile He will more than likely put you in to work that thing out.

Going from puzzled to purpose requires individual puzzling within the area of life you have been sorted. Small groups allow individual pieces to be trained through the process of discovery. Others around you can see how you fit into the vision as you begin to move into place. You will have some trial and error but that is part of the process. It is in these smaller groups that we are being encouraged, perfected and pushed to our potential! When you are fitted into place you are also guiding others to their place, because they can judge where they belong according to where you are positioned. Puzzled people are confused and cause confusion, constantly moving around and not getting settled into who God called them to be. They can sometimes occupy a space not created for them and therefore delaying the growth process all together of those around them. This is selfish because most of the time they occupy these spaces for selfish reasons and not to edify the body of Christ. A puzzled person will see what someone else has and has worked hard to discover and will try to take the short cut to connection. It becomes obvious when this happens because the piece will eventually show a gap (although slight sometimes) in the connection. A puzzled person in the wrong place can also cause a tight fit bending others around them out of shape. This is also selfish! There is a place designed for us to fit in the body of Christ, into God's vision for our lives according to His overall purpose. It will require more than just showing up. It will require willingness to be worked, moved, pushed, turned and connected in areas you may not have considered. God's ways are above our ways and His thoughts are above our thoughts.

Isaiah 55:8-9 NIV
"For my thoughts are not your thoughts, neither are your ways my ways, declares the Lord. 9: As the heavens are higher than the earth, so are my ways higher than your ways and my thoughts than your thoughts."

We must trust and believe Him. Take Him at His word. People who are puzzling are people with purpose and they share the ability to discover new ways of thinking and doing things until the assurance of success is in sight. A person with a "puzzling" mentality succeeds against all odds because they believe. They work together through this connecting process to do the work of the Lord. They are the solution carriers to our economic issues, our family concerns, the marriage crisis and financial hardships. Puzzlers are creative, committed and inspiring to those around them to keep focused on the vision. I think you are beginning to understand the difference now. Don't be fooled into thinking being puzzled is the same as someone who is puzzling. Being puzzled is a state of mind. On the contrary, puzzling is an action- oriented state, a verb, something you do. You will continue to find vast differences between the two thought processes if you look close enough. Don't allow yourself to get in the rut of being puzzled in any area of your life. Being puzzled and not connecting is not where God wants you to spend your time. Now ask yourself, have you been puzzled lately or are you puzzling.

Chapter Six

REFER BACK TO THE VISION

"I don't want to pick up my life on lay- away after I get to Heaven, I want to be used of God to the fullest today!"
Tasha Hart

I recently took a leadership class at my church and during one of the sessions, our Pastor reminded us of the importance of vision. Vision is what gives us hope for our future. That is why in Jeremiah 29:11 God reminds us that He has a plan for us.

Jeremiah 29:11 NIV
"For I know the plans I have for you, declares the Lord, plans to prosper you and not to harm you, plans to give you hope and a future."

The plan and purpose for your life is visible when you allow God to show you piece by piece how to access it. It is that plan of God, that vision that gives us hope. When you feel like you are slipping backward into a puzzled or confused state, stop and remind yourself of this verse in (Jeremiah 29:11), For I know the plans I have for you, plans not to harm you, plans to prosper you, plans to give you a hope and a future. Notice in this verse, it says PLANS, plural! He has plans for you. There are multiple things for you to do in the Kingdom. You have your piece of the puzzle that has areas cut away to allow others to pour into your purpose. Then there are areas of your piece of the puzzle jutting out in order for you to pour your gifts and talents into others, all the while connecting the vision. You find your purpose throughout this connecting process in all areas of your life. There are multiple visions and plans that you will be a part of, if you're willing to be worked, moved and connected. The vision for your marriage will be different from the vision for your family and so forth with other areas of your life. The good news is God has all of the plans worked out for you already. The very fact that God has a plan for my life gives me hope. Doesn't it you? I lay down at night dreaming of the possibilities. I wake up in the morning looking for my daily connection. Where can God use me today? How can I make an impact toward the vision He has for me and toward those in my areas of influence? This alone will keep your eyes open, your fingers writing, your head learning, your ears hearing and your spirit tasting.

Psalm 34:8 NIV
"Taste and see that the Lord is good; blessed is the one who takes refuge in him."

In the King James Version of this verse, it starts out with, "Oh" taste and see and I like that. Don't just taste and see, truly enjoy who God is. A good God who loves you, has plans to prosper you and to give you a hope and a future that you will see His vision for your existence. Earlier we discussed that your piece of the puzzle was not an after-thought. The vision wasn't created and then pieces created to fill in the gaps. We were the vision and still are! No matter the circumstances of my birth or the background I come from or the experiences I've had, I was and am apart of the vision God has for the Kingdom, the body of Christ, His church! God had a plan, not an accident. He didn't just crash one day and decide afterward that He needed to order more parts to fix what He already had. We were planned and strategically designed to connect His vision for a family.

It is easy to get lost in the shuffle during the connecting process if you are not focused on the vision. You can spend a lot of time doing more moving than connecting. I explained in the last chapter that we want to be more than hearers of the Word. We want to be doers, however if all we are doing is moving then we still have missed our purpose. With all our hearing and all our moving are we getting understanding and making the connections we were created for? When we are asking ourselves this question about getting understanding, it's important to refer back to the original vision. Am I prospering in the area I'm currently in? Do I know God has plans for me and am I diligently positioning myself to be used in those plans? Do I have hope in that future? The answer to these questions makes up our vision and keeps us on track toward completing it day-by-day. It is in connecting with others that we are tried and tested and encouraged to accomplish our goals.

In every area of my life I have a vision. I prayed about that vision and asked questions of those around me who know me pretty well. I read books, listened to CDs, watched DVDs and meditated on His Word. I watch the shepherd of my church, our Pastor whom God has appointed over me. Seeking out others with wisdom, I daily press on toward the mark of God's high calling for my spouse, my children, family and me individually. Every day I look for opportunities for God to show me through confirmation or demonstration those things I have read and prayed about are coming to pass. As each day comes, I get more answers, more opportunities and more glimpses of the plans God has for me. It gives me hope! I know I have a future in the Kingdom of God and when doubt tries to creep in, I refer back to the vision.

How does this vision form? It is in the everyday relationship you have with the Father. The routine I described above is not a one-time thing. The way you live your life determines the way you will see and receive vision and purpose. I used to spend a lot of time doing my own thing and adding God to my plans later. God created me to be a leader and a doer of the Word through artistic and creative talents. It is easy for me to get sidetracked onto a good idea. So many ideas have come to my mind and I have attempted to develop a few. Each time I would carefully plan what steps I could take to make that idea or that project a success. Each time I would have a measure of success but ultimately that idea or project would run its course and end.

Just over a year ago, my husband and I decided I should do something I'm passionate about and try to make a business out of it. This would be creating art and selling it as gifts and home décor through a gallery of sorts. We did everything we could possibly think of to make a real go at it. Joining our local Chamber connected us to other business professionals we thought would help me learn the correct steps to making the business a success. Did you know you can be in wise company, but without the divine connection of God to those with the wisdom you need, you will not be in a position to receive or pour into those individuals? After participating in numerous business workshops, networking events and online training videos we felt confident I was headed in the right direction. There was even a brief interview on one of the local TV stations that broadcasts local events and news. We spent what money we had saved to put on a grand opening event introducing artists, myself included to the general public as a way to get unique gifts and artwork for your homes. I was so determined to succeed! Spending money on a website, business cards, signs, promotional material and the like seemed like an investment at the time. A year or so later, I have a fax machine with no one faxing, a business line with no business and a lot of promotional material left over without anything to promote.

I was left empty and once again seeking my part in the purposes of God. It didn't dawn on me in all that time that I was not referring to the vision God had for my life but rather creating a vision all on my own and then asking God to piece it together for me. Let me tell you, God is NOT responsible for piecing together MY vision for MY life and He won't do that for anyone else either. It is no wonder my big ideas have not seen success. Don't misunderstand me, we are a part of the vision process and God wants us to express our desires to Him, but ultimately we have to see if what we are desiring lines up with what He has already desired for us. It would be like a single piece to a puzzle going to its creator and saying, 'I know I was created with this vision in mind but can you move me to another puzzle because I think I would fit over there a little better?'. To the creator that would be ridiculous! You can't take a piece from one vision and transfer it to another and expect it to fit yet we ask this of God all the time. I truly believe God will use my creative talents as I'm connected to His vision and my purpose in this world. However I will be referring back to God's vision so it can be utilized and worked the way it was originally intended. I think I will have much more success this way with ideas in the future.

When you are open to God and the things He has for your life remember not to just ask to be moved but rather allow God to move you where He desires you to be. Don't just work toward a goal but rather be open to whatever God wants to work out in you and through you for His goal in your life. When you are unsure of why you are working on a certain goal or why you are moved into certain areas, refer back to the vision. Look at the glimpses God has given you through connecting with others, your study times, experiences, etc., and remind yourself of where God is leading you.

If you have ever attempted and possibly completed a decent sized puzzle, you have already discovered the importance of referring back to the vision. A puzzle that contains 500 plus pieces can be a challenge to put together. It would be even more difficult to connect all of those pieces if there wasn't a clue as to how the end result should look. This is how God was illustrating vision to me. We all gather together, some of us unwilling to even leave the box. Some of us in sorted piles however not willing to get close and build connecting relationships. Some of us even fall off the table and stay hidden until that time when our piece is needed and the search is on for the missing piece.

Others have been sorted and connected but as they have made their connection they wait on the others to get into place so the vision can be completed. Depending on your viewpoint, it may seem as if this is one chaotic mess! However if you have an overall vision, what appears to be chaotic is actually charismatic. There is a method to the madness so to speak. That lost piece will be found because God the Master puzzler will not rest until the vision is complete! When it comes time for that piece to play its part, it will be sought out.

You may be asking yourself about now how do you know the glimpses you are receiving and seeking are truly from God? How do you know if what you are working toward is truly the vision God has for you? I have heard many people ask that question in various manners but it all comes down to the same thing. People want to know it is God not someone else or they themselves trying to do their own thing. We looked at one situation in my life earlier where I had limited success because I was doing my own thing with my vision in mind. That vision was unable to be completed. A puzzler will often look on the front of the box to get a good look at the vision. The vision will guide them as to where that next piece should fit or the area they will eventually be worked into. Depending on the size of the puzzle the puzzler will have to refer back to that image on the front of the box quite often, piece-by- piece, section-by-section. I have worked puzzles from 300 pieces to over a thousand and when you have that many pieces to work with each individual piece becomes more important to the vision. I put together this puzzle with the picture of a farm once. I don't remember what the size of this one was but I believe it was maybe around 1000 pieces or more. First I took all the pieces out of the box and then I began to flip all the pieces over being careful not to accidentally send one piece flying off the table in haste in order to get a good look at each piece. Immediately I began to pull all the pieces out that had an edge so I could then begin to make my border. This didn't really require me to look at the front of the box because there are fewer edge pieces that make up the border compared to the remainder of the puzzle, however when it is time to get to the inner workings of the puzzle I have to slow down. Looking closer at each piece individually, I picked a pile and began to work it. This pile I was working had many little orange pieces and at a glance you would think how do I distinguish one orange piece from the other in order to connect them? That is when I had to refer back to the front of the box for guidance. I noticed that one orange piece has a brown stem. Then I notice on the front of the box that the brown stem is connected to an orange area with a green vine. As I looked closer those orange pieces really are unique and by carefully connecting them the vision of pumpkins began to take shape. Did the pumpkins always exist or were they created before my eyes? I believe the pumpkins were always there, I just had to refer back to the box to see what the creator of the picture already knew.

This is what happens when we allow God to show us the vision He has and that we want for our future. Sometimes we may not know what it is we are connecting but nonetheless there is something taking place during that connection that is extremely important to the overall vision. Looking back at the front of the box made it easier for me to see that there was a purpose for each piece. There was a reason for the shape of that piece of the puzzle, the color of it and its size. The key was looking at the front of the box and using it as a guide.

As Christians, our front of the box is the Holy Bible. Just like a puzzle box contains all the pieces you need to complete the picture, God's Holy Word contains all the pieces we need to complete His vision. Everything we need to know pertaining to the vision God has for our life is contained within His Word in the Holy Bible. I know this has been said and taught many times, but do you believe that? If you believe it, are you practicing what you believe? Do you pick up your Bible and search out the vision for each area of your life? Do you take the time to connect? As you read His Word, the pieces to your vision will leave the pages. That next piece to the puzzle will come to you and allow you to connect various areas of your life that give purpose to your existence. What are you believing for, when you open the Bible? There are pieces in those pages you were meant to find and those pieces will connect for you in a way they won't for anyone else. Are you allowing the Bible to be your guide that points you to God's vision for your life? Do you trust Him? If the answer is yes, have you noticed each chapter in this book to this point comes down to a decision on our part? Every chapter leaves you with a question regarding what you may or may not be willing to do I'm excited for those of us who are eager to say yes to every question? Will you leave your comfort zone? Yes! Will you allow the Father to examine you closely and work out any areas of your life? Yes! This chapter poses the question, will you refer back to God's vision for your life or your own? What kind of life are you living and what is that kind of life guided by? I don't know what your answer is, as for me and my house it will forever be, Yes! And Amen! We will live out the life God has planned and refer back to His vision often.

I have gotten ahead of God at times and pushed ahead without referring back to His vision. I can hear myself in a conversation with God as I eagerly take over, convincing myself that I am just showing my enthusiasm and appreciation for what God has for me. Actually, I was over confident! I had everything figured out; I was eager to "prove" myself to others and to God that I was "worthy" of this opportunity. This is NOT what God has in mind when He gives us pieces to the vision. As He begins to work us, revelation and knowledge comes. It is to be guarded and processed like everything else in our lives. You don't eat raw meant without preparing it first for consumption. I am embarrassed to say I've done just that. I've take the raw meat of God's Word for my life and eaten it without preparing it first. This only caused delays, as I had to get over the sickness of disappointment and regret. Don't eat the raw vision God has for your life. Prepare it, season it and allow the goodness that awaits you to come forth.

On the other hand, don't overcook the vision. Referring back to the vision is the same as following instructions. You take it one step at a time being careful not to skip steps or rush the process. My grandmother was an excellent cook. She could afford to skip some steps in the kitchen. She didn't always have to use a measuring cup or follow the instructions exactly. She knew from experience what had to happen to make her meals just right. God works with us by instructing us on His vision by His Word. He knows exactly what we need and how we need to prepare. He is the only one that knows the shortcuts and exceptions to the rules. We can't take something we don't have experience in and just skip steps and make up our own way of putting it all together. It won't work! The instructions are there. Read them. The Holy Spirit is our teacher, allow Him to guide you and He will.

The vision is not just a picture on the front of a puzzle box, it is the heart of the Father. He is the only one who knows what the entire picture looks like. I don't know about you but I get excited about that very thought. I am one piece to a giant puzzle that is painted on the heart of the Father. I matter to His purposeful vision for family and connection and so do you. What is it that makes you who you are? I no longer ask myself questions like why don't I belong or fit here or there. Instead I am grateful for the moving process, the sorting and interaction as I find myself pouring into others and them doing the same for me. As I refer back to the vision and try connecting various pieces, I will always find some pieces just don't fit into certain areas. No longer do I force pieces together or get frustrated that I haven't connected the right pieces at that time. I look at the elimination process as a success. For every piece that doesn't fit or doesn't make a connection, I am that much closer to the one that does. As I continue referring back to the vision, I become quicker at sorting and connecting pieces as I go because the vision starts to become imprinted in my mind and on my heart. Some areas I have referred back to so often I have memorized what that part of the vision looks like. I know what I'm looking for in that area. Careful now, I'm starting to sound like a master puzzler. Referring back to the vision can sharpen your skills as a puzzler of life. You don't have to spend as much time in areas as you used to because you keep the vision close and if something doesn't fit you can quickly move on. You will find this very productive as you move on to puzzling various areas of your life.

As I said in the beginning, this idea of puzzling and going from puzzled to purpose can work in many facets. What do I mean? This book is just meant to open your eyes to the possibilities and strategies of connection in the body of Christ for God's vision and purpose for your life. As you begin to grasp these strategies and apply them to different areas of your life such as marriage or parenting you will find yourself mastering your ability to quickly decide if one piece of the puzzle fits into that vision or not and move on. You will find your life connecting in ways you never dreamed possible. This doesn't mean you will have all the answers but that you believe there IS an answer. You just have to be dedicated to the vision and regardless if some pieces don't fit where you want them to you, stay committed to the overall process. Once again I've know people who have quit right here. They didn't like the fact that their wife couldn't be the lead singer in the worship band so they quit the vision all together and decided that because that one piece didn't fit we have to get a whole new vision. This is just an example but I hope you get the point. Why not just move that one piece into the area of the vision it belongs and keep pressing toward all God has for you in that area? Don't keep starting over vision after vision after vision and never resolving to see one through to completion. Get into the Word of God, Get that vision and begin working it with God piece-by-piece. Don't get discouraged when a piece doesn't fit when or where you want it to, but be excited that you have eliminated a possibility and that allowed you to get one piece closer to the final picture. The heart of the Father is beating. It is thumping at the thought of you getting closer. He loves you and I. He wants us to get this. He wants us to include Him in the process. It is ultimately His vision for us, so just ask Him to show you what to do and where to connect.

Refer back to the vision! Let it be your guide to what God is calling you toward. It will show you where you need to be placed and how you fit into the plans God has for your life and those you connect with.

Chapter Seven

REACHING OUT

"I've learned to be an opportunity for others rather than ask others for an opportunity."

Tasha Hart

Once you are well on your way to the area of the puzzle you belong you will begin to see where you will assist others in finding their fit. So far we have focused on ourselves individually connecting and finding our own fit. The puzzle doesn't stop there. As we Christians find our fit it is imperative we seek out those who also need to find their place in the vision. Where is that piece with the crooked side and narrow cut away? I think I see where that piece fits in. When you are positioned where you need to be, it becomes easier to see what pieces need to go where.

You are a part of the vision and when others refer back to the vision to find their place they are not only reading the Word as a guide they are referring back to those around them already in place. This is why it is key for us to find our fit and do it diligently so others can find their place as well. Often times when I am completing a puzzle I refer back to the front of the box and we discussed that this is similar to referring back to the Bible for God's vision. Then there are times when I look around at the pieces already fitted in place and compare them to the piece I am currently working with to see how it connects. This is what I call reaching out. I am already fitted in place and I can reach out to others to help them find their fit. I can walk them through the process I took to get where I am and show them how to do the same. Eventually, as pieces are added to the existing connected pieces of the puzzle, the vision begins to expand toward completion. There is timesaving productivity in sharing the vision and conveying instructions. This just means that because I am firmly planted where I belong and I'm not moving, you can take a risk and see if you and I have a connection. You can move yourself around my area so to speak and see if you fit.

There will be various opportunities for connection depending on the area of your life God is working on with you. If it's marriage for example and there is another couple in your church who is firmly planted in that area and their marriage is similar to the vision God has for your marriage He may have you connect with this couple. Because this couple was firmly planted, you could see them in place and make a quick assessment whether or not connection could begin through them. The process of piecing that vision together in that area of your life would require you taking a risk to see if that is the next piece to the vision in developing a better marriage. If you keep doing this over and over again, you will realize that growth is taking place. It is amazing to see how each area of the vision gets larger and larger until some areas begin to touch. One area will begin to affect another area as we each do our part. The edge of the puzzle doesn't seem so far away and the center is no longer in the distance.

I laugh when I look back over my life and realize how many times I tried to complete a vision God gave me on my own. I can't be the border, the center and the connecting pieces all by myself! I have to be willing to share the vision with others and reach out to those who also play a part in bringing the vision to pass.

It is common for people to think that this connecting thing is easy and pretty normal in the body of Christ, but I think that it is in the body that connecting needs improvement. The world has no problem reaching out to those that will further their agenda, career or personal endeavors. People are pulled into social circles all the time in order to expand the impact of that group. I believe now is the time for Christians to catch up to this reaching out and connecting process. We can't afford to lose viable pieces to God's vision because they simply haven't been pulled in. Even worse we have not firmly planted ourselves and committed to the vision in front of us as Christians, so when others arrive they don't have a clear since of what they might be getting into--what they may be connecting with. It is up to us that have already found our fit to be used to guide others into their place. We have to commit to the vision God has for our lives as individuals, as a church body, as a family, as husband and wife, etc. It's simple really. Point them to the Word and refer them back to the vision as we reach out to them. I know this works because I see how it has changed the lives of those connected around me and I have experienced this for myself.

After the failure of the business I mentioned earlier and some countless other attempts to succeed on various levels in my life, I began to lose hope. Even as Christians, if we are not referring back to the vision and we are not focused on allowing God to guide us to where we fit in, it is easy to find ourselves alone and disconnected. For a Christian, this is a very dangerous place to be. To know the hope you once had and lose it can be devastating and can open the door for the enemy to send you spiraling into a world of loneliness, depression, anger and defeat. Let's not have another expensive heart surgery! Keep it moving. I was experiencing this kind of frustration when a group of women referring back to the vision God had given them, reached out to me. They pointed me to the Word of God and reminded me that I do have a position in God's vision for not only my individual life but for the body of Christ as well. There is power in connecting and that connecting happens when others are willing to reach out. This same group of women has repeated this reaching out process and in turn has opened the doors of possible connection among those who may have stayed in that "puzzled" mindset.

We have to be willing to give of ourselves so that we ourselves can be instruments of connection. This is how God is connecting His family. This happens when willing pieces of the vision are properly positioned and ready to pull in the other missing pieces. This allows the vision to grow and expand toward its purpose. I am now a part of the reaching out process.

I don't have the full vision figured out but I do have a strategy to stay connected. I trust God will continue increasing the vision piece by piece as I continue reaching out to others for His Glory. It is not about me. I know God is going to use my shape, my color, size, personality, character, etc., to connect with others and reach out to those that haven't connected to God's vision thus far.

Those they may find themselves "puzzled" and unsure of the next piece in the vision God has for their lives are about to go from puzzled to purpose. This is the time for the body of Christ to be strengthened in their inner man that together they can move forward into the greater things of God. This reaching out has to be real, sincere and in love. Many things in this world are pulling for our time and pulling for our attention and many of those things are loveless, hopeless and lifeless. As we begin to reach out to those that need this connection to God we have to be sincere and do it out of love. That is also part of the vision. God is love.

1 John 4:8 NIV
"Whoever does not love does not know God, because God is love."

I have felt this loveless outreach in my life and it left me feeling even more hopeless and alone. Once when I was in my early twenties, I had this overwhelming feeling of just being completely and utterly alone. This feeling so overwhelmed me that I went to the closest church near my home and went inside. This church was not my church home but it was open during the day to the public. No one asked me any questions as I made my way through the foyer to the sanctuary. The lights were out in the sanctuary as I made my way toward the front. There on the second pew I sat down and began to cry. That didn't do much for me except make me sleepy and so I fell asleep across the pew. Yes this church still had pews. It reminded me of my childhood in that small town with the little white house on the corner I described in the beginning of this book.

The church I was raised and baptized in as a child had pews similar to the one I was lying on. It made me feel close to home for a moment. I don't know if I dreamed this or if it was a visual thought when I woke up but God answered my prayer. Before I had fallen asleep and after I had stopped crying I wanted to know why I always felt alone. All my life it seemed I was the odd person out, at school, with my friends and even among my own family. I could see myself standing inside a room with a big window in front of me. The window had many of those little square panes like the kind you see on storefronts at Christmastime. It was winter and as I was looking out this huge window into the street outside when I noticed that Jesus was beside me looking out into the street as well. There were men, women and children all bundled up hustling and bustling about their day. From my perspective it appeared these people had a life full of purpose with people to see and places to go while I was standing on the inside of this room alone, looking out on the world. I can almost laugh at myself as I tell this story to you now. During this moment, I remember Jesus saying to me that the yearning I had to be a part of the lives of those people came from Him. Clueless as to what Jesus was trying to show me I again went back to how I felt and reminded Jesus that I'd rather stay inside this room with Him and never go out there again where people won't accept me and I'm constantly facing this feeling of loneliness. Jesus didn't look at me because He was still gazing out of the window, but He said that He deals with rejection from people all the time but it doesn't stop the desire for Him to have their attention and their heart. Then He reminded me that inside me I carried the Kingdom. I had on the inside of me God the Father, Jesus the Son and the Holy Spirit.

John 14:23 NIV
"Jesus replied, "Anyone who loves me will obey my teaching. My Father will love them, and we will come to them and make our home with them."

2 Timothy 1:14 NIV
"Guard the good deposit that was entrusted to you-guard it with the help of the Holy Spirit who LIVES in us."

I learned through me, His willing vessel, I would carry the family of the trinity out to connect with the people in those streets. I am to bring the family of the Trinity to others by building relationships and engaging in interactions with those I come in contact with. I can't do that if I stay inside this room with Jesus. It is not only unfulfilling but selfish. You might think to yourself, how can being alone with Jesus in a room be unfulfilling. There are moments we need to be alone with Jesus, God our Father and the Holy Spirit, but in those moments it is usually for our own personal needs. This is okay but it is not what we were created to do. We were not created to simply exist alone with God. He wants a family and we are a part of that process. I began to look out the window again with a new perspective. That feeling of loneliness began to fade as Jesus reminded me that where I go, I take my family of four with me...Jesus, God, the Holy Spirit and me and they would be there when I introduced myself to someone out there. They wanted me to bring those people to meet the family and join us for dinner sometime.

There are times I need to be refreshed and spend some alone time with my creator however never again will I be foolish enough to think that I am the only one my creator wants and needs to spend time with. His heart is my heart and that heart wants to connect with others to expand His family. I have to ask myself in moments like that, where is my focus. If my focus is on Christ and His heart for His people then I can't afford the luxury of staying cut off from my purpose. God answers our prayers through the people we connect and interact with on a daily basis. If I am keeping to myself and frustrated with the world so much I refuse to make connections then I am not only going to fail at reaching out to others who are in need but the ones God sent to reach out to me will not find me to connect with either. I can't be that missing piece of the puzzle forever.

The enemy would love for us to stay in a state of selfish loneliness and blame it on all THOSE people out there. All THOSE people who hurt us but we can't do that without looking beside ourselves to see Jesus. Can you stand beside Him day-after-day and continue to give Him the same excuse as to why you can't leave this lonely place and get out there to do the work of His high calling. Can you turn away from your own feelings of doubt, hurt and disappointment to look over at Jesus gazing out of the window at His lost people? Can you tell Jesus to His face that today is not the day? Today you choose your vision. If we don't go out to reach the lost pieces, we keep Jesus cooped up in the walls of our selfish hearts and the Bible says in (Mark 16:15) to go into all the world and preach the Gospel.

Mark 16:15 NIV
"He said to them, Go into all the world and preach the gospel to all creation."

For the Glory of God I will go out into the world, I will ask, I will seek, I will connect and share the Gospel so that the heart of my Creator is satisfied. It is through connecting that I find purpose and fulfillment in my life. As we all reach out to connect, there is someone coming alongside me to gird me up and hold me accountable to my calling. There is strength in numbers and that strength comes from continuing to expand the Kingdom Vision of God. Don't allow the world to send you running inside to hide from your purpose. Get the courage to see what God sees and then reach out to expand the vision for family with love through our Savior Jesus Christ.

Chapter Eight

Progress

"A toddler doesn't ask permission to walk and I decided I shouldn't either."

Tasha Hart

I am thankful to my Father in Heaven that success in His kingdom is not based on progress in this world's system. How can we stay in hope if we can't see progress in our purpose? It is one thing to know we have a purpose, that we belong to the body of Christ and have a place in His family. It is a completely different thing to move beyond just knowing and into actively seeing that purpose in Christ progressing. What good is it for a pianist to learn notes and melodies if they never play a tune? How can an artist feel fulfilled in their abilities if they never complete a work of art? It is seeing progression in what we were created to do that brings us closer to the hope of the high calling that is within us. That high calling is not in and of our selves but in and of Christ Jesus.

Philippians 3:4-14 NIV

"Though I myself have reasons for such confidence. If someone else thinks they have reasons to put confidence in the flesh, I have more: 5: circumcised on the eighth day, of the people of Israel, of the tribe of Benjamin, a Hebrew of Hebrews; in regard to the law, a Pharisee 6: as for zeal, persecuting the church; as for righteousness based on the law, faultless. 7: But whatever were gains to me I now consider loss for the sake of Christ. 8: What is more, I consider everything a loss because of the surpassing worth of KNOWING Christ Jesus my Lord, for whose sake I have lost all things. I consider them garbage, that I may gain Christ. 9: and be found in him, not having a righteousness of my own that comes from the law, but that which through faith in Christ – the righteousness that comes from God on the basis of faith. 10: I want to know Christ-yes, to know the power of his resurrection and participation in his sufferings, becoming like him in his death, 11: and so, somehow, attaining to the resurrection from the dead. 12: Not that I have already obtained all this, or have already arrived at my goal, but I press on to take hold of that for which Christ Jesus took hold of me. 13: Brothers and sisters, I do not consider myself yet to have taken hold of it. But one thing I do: Forgetting what is behind and straining toward what is ahead, 14: I press on toward the goal to win the prize for which God has called me heavenward in Christ Jesus."

Our success is not in achieving by the world's standard but in believing in Christ Jesus. Read this scripture again and let that sink in. Are you chasing after a purpose or chasing after the Christ who gives purpose to you?

Society tells us from an early age to progress and succeed in life. The problem is most of the time the measure of our progress is based on the world's idea of success. I learned at a very early age that if I wanted to succeed I had to work hard and figure out how this system works for myself.

I remember one summer I wanted to go on a trip to the amusement park. Coming from a small town like the one I grew up in, going on a bus trip anywhere was amusing enough. I remember the weeks leading up to the trip the various kids and some adults were talking about how the bus trip was going to be so much fun you did not want to miss out. I knew that my parents could not afford for my siblings or I to go on this trip.

The need to figure out a plan and make this trip a reality pushed my mind into gear. I had a plan. I got my siblings, cousins and some childhood friends together to start a coin drive. I drew and colored all these paper flyers about the trip and instructed my recruits on what to say to our possible supporters. Continuing with the plan, I had them spread out in the parking lot of a local grocery store in shifts for almost an entire day without the knowledge of my parents by the way. The results were a little over $200 dollars. From the appearance of things I'm thinking I'm making progress toward my goal and this little plan was a success. What I didn't plan on was my parents finding out. One of our "supporters" was a friend of my father's who decided to call him at work and let him in on our day's activities. I got home where my father was waiting for me and wanted to know "whose" big idea this was? My father didn't like the idea of his children out on the streets begging for money that he went to work for everyday and worked hard to get. I was ashamed that I had made this elaborate plan to supply my own needs when my father wanted to be the provider for me. I embarrassed him but he forgave me. He did make me turn that change over to the church. The point of this story is to simply say, my idea of success, progress and accomplishments were not the same as my father's. What looks like progress to me, is not my father's view of progress. I have to be careful to stay focused on my father, allow him to direct my life and seek THE Father for provision and true progress in His Kingdom. For all intents and purposes this idea I had didn't seem so bad at the time. In my eyes I was saving my father the hassle and embarrassment of not being able to come up with the money for me to go on this bus trip with the church. More than once I have found myself in this same position with God. Without giving Him the opportunity to provide for me I begin coming up with excuses as to why I have to provide for myself. I tell myself that I have all I need so a want is not necessary for God to get involved with. Then I've also convinced myself that I'm doing God a favor by saving Him the trouble of having to prove to one more person that He can make something happen for my good and that He can do anything. These ideas were actually blocking me from the truth. God has already progressed in every area of my life. He began a good work in me and has already brought it to completion before I could ask for the provision. If I would put all my focus on Him instead of actually making results happen I would see progress in my purpose.

The idea is to know that progress is always IN progress all you have to do is be progressing! Now say that two times faster! All that means is if I'm connecting and focusing on God, one day I'll look up. This is where I want us to STOP. Think about that statement. Our Father who is in heaven cares about everything concerning us. He cares about what we care about and to "save Him the hassle of caring" is simply ridiculous. He loves us too much to even count our little cares a hassle. It is in our "little cares" that we find out who we are and whose we are and what we were created to be.

What does this have to do with progress? We HAVE to realize and accept what we were created to do and that usually ties into what we are passionate about or what we truly CARE about. What we are passionate about usually creates the "little cares" of our life. For example, I love art and anything that has to do with creating, painting, drawing or bringing the imagination to life. In my world that passion for art is what creates the "little cares" in my life. If Hobby Lobby is having a sale on paper, I'm the one breaking the piggy bank and busting the door down to get my hands on as many colors and textures as I can. If I don't have enough funds to take advantage of the entire sale it saddens me a little. I settle for what I can afford but deep inside I feel a little "squish" happening on my heart of hearts. Why? I am thinking of all the possibilities of what I can create with what I just acquired and all the people's hearts I can touch with the things I make and to know I can't do that all the time, as much as I want hurts a little. To the average person this does not seem like a big deal. People ask me quite often, what are you going to do with that? They ask me this question because they don't see the possibilities that I see. They don't really care about all "that" the way I do. This is the opposite of how a person who was created to create things with their hands and imagination feels. It's what I truly care about and I use those little cares to touch lives and to me that is a very big deal. When I am not creating I don't feel like I'm seeing progress take place in the person God created me to be. He created me to be a creator and use my creativity to touch others. For someone else it could be their ability to touch people's lives with their cooking or their singing. Now cooking is one gift I enjoy receiving but I'm not good at dishing out, and singing, I enjoy it but it's not "my thing" so to speak. You might have been expecting something more profound but it's that simple. Purpose is all tied up in perfecting the little cares that God has put inside you and doing it for the Glory of God. It is there you will find your purpose progressing and giving hope to others and in turn giving hope to you.

When I'm not doing what I love I feel hopeless and a vicious cycle of disappointment and idle thoughts begin. I am not focused on God, I am not focused on who I am; I am not focused on whose I am and what I was created to do. Without progression in my purpose I am left feeling unfulfilled and empty. How do I get out of this vicious cycle? How do I move from the world's system of progress to the progression of purpose in God way of doing things? The world tells me that if I am not actively productive I am a failure. This thought got me thinking about why my purpose was so important to me in the first place. I genuinely want to live a life of purpose because it pleases God to see me doing what He created me to do. It's that simple. I'm love my Father and I want to do what pleases Him more than anything. It is not because I want recognition from the world so they can pat me on my back and welcome me into the club of success. I want to be wrapped in my Father's arms and hear His heartbeat and know that I made it race a little. That somehow in all the ways that I can with everything I am and was created to be demonstrates the love I have for Him. It is all I have to offer. Now that sounds really sweet doesn't it? I'm not kidding, it does sound sweet and I meant every word but here is where some Christians get sidetracked. It isn't about me, remember? It isn't about you either! It is about our God and if what I said above is truly how I feel then I will seek out what really pleases Him. It isn't our sweet words or good intentions. It is our faith! Scripture tells us this is fact ladies and gents! In Hebrews 11:6 you will see that faith is what pleases God.

Hebrews 11:6
"And without faith it is impossible to please God, because anyone who comes to him must believe that he exists and that he rewards those who earnestly seek him."

So I ask you today, do you have faith enough in who God created you to be to go after your purpose? Don't say yes because you have read one more book that makes you feel good. It is not about you and it's not based on how you feel.

It is simply living to please God and knowing that living by faith is the way to do it. I can't give up, even when I feel like it because I love God too much and I know His heart beats for His people and I want to be a part of the thump, thump, thump in the Father's chest when He sees His vision coming to pass for a family that is connected. Don't get me wrong and misunderstand what I am saying. Faith is how we please Him but we must show our faith with love because remember God IS love.

1 John 4:8 NIV
"Whoever does not love does not know God, because God is love."

In 1 Corinthians 13:2 we can clearly see that love is key to operating in our faith. Don't just serve God to get recognition or to check off a list of do's and don'ts. Serve Him to please Him because you love Him and because He first loved you and I. There are many who don't know about this love and through our active faith we can demonstrate this truth. We can do this with purpose and truly be someone in Christ.

1 Corinthians 13:2 NIV
"If I have the gift of prophecy and can fathom all mysteries and all knowledge, and if I have a faith that can move mountains, but do not have love, I am nothing."

This scripture takes away the argument that we should count ourselves as nothing and just be lowly in life. This is false! Why would scripture say without love, I am nothing if being nothing was nothing to concern ourselves with? If being nothing was a non- issue why bring it up? We were all created to BE SOMETHING! Without faith and without love our ability to connect to our purpose and please God is impossible. You have to have both just like in a marital relationship. You can't have a good marriage if there isn't love and faith.

There is that popular song called, "Love and Marriage" and in that song it says you can't have one without the other. You can say it like this "Faith and Love" you can't have one without the other. I wouldn't want to marry someone who loved me if he couldn't be faithful. God doesn't want anything less from us. Don't serve Him in faith if you can't love and don't just love if you can't have faith. God is love and you please Him loving others by faith. This answers a lot of your questions whether you realize it or not. When you are deciding daily what to do with your time and talents or determining if something is about to please God, put that action on the love and faith scale. Ask yourself if what you are about to do, say, think, create, etc., demonstrates the love of God? Will it require faith to bring it about in the full scale you envision? I think God will be pleased if you answer yes to both of those questions. If you are getting a lot of yes answers to this daily question I'm confident in saying to you that you are probably operating in your purpose or getting pretty close to it. Either way you won't be on the sidelines wishing you were connecting in the body of Christ.

The world's foundation for measuring success is not accurate for a believer. The world's system for measuring success is determined by the world's currency. If you have a lot of money and possessions you are considered successful by worldly standards. The thought behind this is that the more you have acquired in wealth the more you must be fulfilling your purpose in life. You are pushed to progress and succeed. The issue is that the world pushes us to compare ourselves to our neighbor, our family members, friends, our bosses and coworkers in all areas of our lives in order to measure our levels of success. The system of comparison does not compare to God's system built on love through Christ Jesus. Money is the world's currency that gives us access to success by the world's standard. In the Kingdom of God, faith is the currency that gives us access to ALL things we need to succeed by God's standards. This currency of faith gains us access to more than just money it gives us access to ALL things pertaining to life and success in the Kingdom of Heaven. It takes faith to love the way we should and demonstrate that love through our purpose and the more faith we have the more love we can demonstrate. It is our faith that can be measured according to the Bible. Just like money can be counted and increased our faith has the ability to increase as well. You can be rich in faith utilizing your faith "currency" to access all you need to be successful in your purpose.

1 John 4:8 NIV
"Whoever does not love does not know God, because God is love."

Luke 17:5-6 NIV
"The apostles said to the Lord, "Increase our faith!"
6: He replied, "If you have faith as small as a
mustard seed, you can say to this mulberry tree, "Be
uprooted and planted in the sea," and it will obey
you."

If our faith was not able to increase the disciples would not have asked Jesus the question and in turn Jesus would not have given them an answer. It is also interesting to note that Jesus didn't ignore the fact that the faith they currently had was the key to their increase. The "little faith" they had, had the power to uproot a mulberry tree but by that one action the disciples would see how strong their faith truly was and therefore by exercising that faith, consequently their faith would increase to do bigger and greater things. Our faith can increase, so I ask you, how much faith do you have today and is it increasing? We have little time left to stay stagnant in places we don't belong comparing ourselves to others when there is no comparison. Your progress is in your ability to trust Him more. Your progress is in the everyday ability to stretch your faith and believe for more than you did the day before. Your progress is your ability to BELIEVE.

In my story about the coin drive I did not for one second consider my father could afford the trip. I did not trust that he could provide my hearts desire. I can say that often I have taken that same attitude with God.

I didn't trust that He could provide for my needs let alone the desires of my heart. I have worked most of my life trying to keep up, fit in, get ahead and all the while my Father has been trying to show me this process of connection. The desires of my heart can be met by faith through Christ for His vision that I have a purpose in bringing to completion.

If you are increasingly growing in your trust of the Lord and allowing that trust to build your faith and in turn using that faith to believe for the things God has put on your heart, you are LIVING in your purpose, and THAT is progress! As you see the desires of your heart begin to move in a forward motion. The act of seeing the desires of your heart begin to take place will stretch your faith to believe a little more. Everyday you wake up with the desire to see more of God in more areas of your life you are progressing in your purpose.

1 Peter 4:10 NIV
"Each of you should use whatever gift you have received to serve others, as faithful stewards of God's grace in its various forms."

We are told in scripture to use our gifts to serve one another. Progress is defined as a forward or onward movement toward a destination according to Webster's New World Dictionary for Young Readers. If the desire of your heart moves you forward toward the destination of the Father's heart you will find He will connect you with others along the way. Who wants to travel alone? I think about people who are satisfied where they are and have that hometown mentality. This is not necessarily a bad thing but there are some people who have stopped along the path of progress and decided they no longer wanted to move forward toward their destination. This is not okay if you are continually seeking the heart of the Father. Even if you never leave your "hometown" leave the mentality behind. Always be ever progressing forward toward the destination God has set before you. Utilize the gifts and abilities He has given you to connect with others, serve others and move toward the heart of the Father. Remember the metaphor of the puzzle and realize that God has an overhead view of the final picture. He placed you in a position that would help the vision continue forward toward completion. The progress you see depends on the trust you have in God and your ability to have faith in the connecting process to fulfill your purpose. Do not get too comfortable until the vision of God is complete and just when He has completed the vision in one area of your life, He opens another box.

I don't mention progress the way the world mentions success. I mention progress to encourage you to look for the fruit of your labor. Bearing fruit for the Kingdom is encouraging. It lets us know we are growing in Christ and we are doing what we were created to do, produce, multiply, share and connect others with the Gospel of our Lord and Savior. These are the things our purposed lives bring into manifestation. Through us, Christ operates His Vision by the Holy Spirit all for the Glory of God. YOU have to know that when you start to see this all working for your good and the common good of all you are living the greatest part of your life! Once you experience that kind of progress and that kind of fulfillment you won't turn back to the comfort of the box. You won't stay disconnected from the vision. You will take your place, do your part, connect and see your purpose progressing.

Chapter Nine

Completion

"I didn't start believing that I couldn't do something until I believed someone who told me I couldn't do something. I stopped believing in that someone and decided to believe God."

Tasha Hart

W hen I begin a puzzle, I have to trust that as I begin the process every piece is actually in the box before I begin.

It would be foolish for me to spend countless hours working out a picture that had no possibility of being completed. All through this book we have talked about many things leading up to this one simple truth. God has a plan for you (Jeremiah 29:11) and that plan for you individually is also part of a bigger plan that has nothing to do with you individually but to do with the family of God as a whole. He wants His family together with Him, connected in unity and love. Why? Because He loves us!

There are benefits to finishing a puzzle. Puzzles are used in the educational system to enhance a child's learning experience. From an early age people encourage children to work puzzles from very simplistic ones to the advanced and complicated. A person who considers themselves as a master puzzler, has skills that he or she has built up from the process of repeatedly completing puzzles and learning the process. Puzzles are used throughout society to build our foundation of learning. There are more than jigsaw puzzles that do this but basically they stimulate the brain so that the capacity to learn and understand is continuing in its development. I used to teach pre-school children and we introduced them to puzzles as a way of developing their fine and gross motor skills. Puzzles foster our ability to problem-solve, reason and/or analyze options and information while increasing our ability to form logical thoughts. In order for this problem- solving development to grow, the puzzler has to be aware of the space required to complete the puzzle. God already knows the importance of having space to work and grow. Look at the human body. He has allowed room for our skin and bones and organs to stretch and grow. This is the same with puzzles. In order to see it completed, you have to look ahead and make sure you have given yourself enough space to complete the vision.

If you look at the definition of a kinesthetic learner you will discover they learn best through practical hands-on activities. You may be the same way. Perhaps you work best when you are in the trenches and doing things hands-on. You might be that person who can hardly wait for the Pastor to finish preaching so you can go out and put your hands to what was said.

Some of us have an auditory preference to learning and in this situation that person may prefer to speak about the puzzle and talk about each step as it's being worked. These are the people that want to talk after church and process verbally what has been said and they are the ones who go forth and repeat what was said and search out scriptures to speak up and speak out the good news!

There are also the obvious visual learners who by seeing the puzzle come together have that sense of accomplishment and fulfillment. These are the people who want to see the work completed. They are diligent in sticking with the vision until it has been completed. They have to see it!

No matter the learning style, the example of the puzzle shows you how each can be utilized to get the same result. No matter who you are or what you prefer the goal is to work life, work the problems, solve them using your gifts, talents and abilities in Christ by His Holy Spirit. See the vision of God being worked!

The objective of a puzzle is to demonstrate our ability to solve a problem and show our increasing ability to complete the task-at-hand. Most of the time, the puzzle reinforces something the person already knows. For example, if a child is in preschool and that week they are learning about farm animals, often times the teacher of the class will introduce puzzles containing farm-related things such as animals and farming equipment. The child already knows what farm animals are but the puzzles help develop areas of our abilities such as those mentioned previously concerning our learning methods. This development brings us closer to completing our purpose more effectively and efficiently.

This happens in the body of Christ as well. God will take something we already have some knowledge of and introduce a "puzzle" to further enhance our learning experience in that area. Completing a puzzle shows God where we are at in our development and what we are prepared to take on next. Our puzzles get larger as our ability to handle them increases.

It's funny how a child can put the same puzzle he/she struggled with in the beginning, more quickly after completing the puzzle the first time around. The child starts to remember where this piece goes and that piece goes and the second time around isn't as difficult. Soon, after the child has completed the puzzle for the third, fourth and fifth time the child has become an expert almost completing the puzzle entirely by memory.

This is how God utilizes us in this connecting process. We can help others complete a puzzle we have already had experience in, mastering each step piece-by-piece to bring that vision or plan of God to completion. By showing others how to connect in areas we have already been, we increase the rate of completion for God's family to fulfill their purpose in Him.

In the area of marriage we connect with others who are married for example and we begin to show them the steps of completing God's vision for their marriage one piece at a time. Those who have completed that vision for their lives are well on their way to other areas God has set before them but they are now capable of showing others the way. God utilizes us and works through us to make these connections. We don't do this on our own. Remember who created the puzzle? Remember who has the end vision in sight? Remember who can see the BIG picture? That is whom we rely on to bring all the pieces together.

I have loved solving puzzles since I was a child. I had a neighbor who loved puzzles also. My neighbor, Ms. Delores, was like an aunt to me. Sometimes when my mother had to work late she would wait for me after school and bring me over to her home. I enjoyed these times at her home very much as she would always have a puzzle in the works on a dinner tray or the kitchen table and sometimes both. I remember the first time she challenged me to do a "large" puzzle. At this time in my life, I had never completed a puzzle over 500 pieces. I was a little intimidated by the size of the puzzle and all the pieces that lay before us. She began to show me how you start with the space and by having proper room to lay everything out. Ms. Delores was an expert after completing dozens of puzzles that were over

3,000 pieces. I listened and watched and more importantly, obeyed. I couldn't wait to get home from school and go to see Ms. Delores so we could work on our puzzle. Ms. Delores would be right beside me as I diligently worked the puzzle piece-by-piece, section-by-section. Sometimes I would be working so hard on the puzzle I didn't notice that she had moved off to the other side of the room at times and allowed me to do most of the parts on my own. I could see the picture forming as I connected pieces here and there. When I would get stuck, Ms. Delores would come right over and help me dig through the pieces for what I needed and in the process she taught me what to look for. The most exciting moment took place when that puzzle was finally completed. I finally got it! I could see the entire picture now! Ms. Delores celebrated with me over a bowl of ice cream and we reviewed the entire process. We talked about which areas were difficult and what parts I had to come back to several times and that one piece I put in the wrong section and later had to move it to its proper place. It was finished! Now my ability to complete a puzzle spurred me on to the next puzzle and bigger puzzles since then.

Through this illustration, God reminded me that He is the one who helps me bring my puzzles into completion. He is the one who watches and comes along side to assist me when things are not connecting. He is the one who shows me direction on what areas to work and what pieces need to be moved and finally celebrate the work that has been completed! He loves it when we finally get the vision. When we can see what He sees in us, for us and those we live life with it is an amazing faith-builder. The best part is that I don't have to work the puzzle alone. I am only responsible for working my part of the vision.

Isaiah 46:10 NIV
"I make known the end from the beginning from ancient times, what is still to come. I say, My purpose will stand and I will do all that I please."

It is His vision. God knows the beginning from the end. He knows the vision for all areas of my life, your life and the body of Christ at-large. In Philippians 1:6, we see finishing the work that He started.

Philippians 1:6 NIV
"Being confident of this, that he who began a good work in you will carry it on to completion until the day of Christ Jesus."

Not only is the work good but also, I'm not responsible for it's completion. I'm only responsible to do the work, my part, and my piece of the puzzle as God leads and directs my life. Do you believe God will complete the vision for your life?

Mark 11:24 NIV

"Therefore I tell you, whatever you ask for in prayer, believe that you have received it, and it will be yours."

Simply Ask...

Father,
Let me move from puzzled to purpose in every area of my life. Teach me to work each area section-by-section, piece-by- piece. Help me see the big picture and rely on you to complete the vision for my life that I may know I am fulfilling my purpose in the body of Christ. Let me continue to connect to those you want me to help along the way and send those I need to connect with that I also may continue moving forward toward the heart of you, Father. Amen.

Connecting to Continue...

Today I believe that God is still the same yesterday, today and forever. Today I also believe that just like in times passed God is moving. It's not that He ever stops moving but sometimes there is a wave that comes when He moves and that is what I am feeling. All over the body of Christ I believe others are feeling this wave as well. It's a strengthening of our spiritual muscles. It brings maturity to the believer and activates us in our purpose if we haven't been fully operating in it this far. Just like a soldier assigned to ACTIVE duty I believe the body of Christ is being called to be just that. ACTIVE! There is an awakening and as the body begins to loosen its limbs, stretch its muscles and shake off the numbness the enemy is aware. The enemy is coming to steal, kill and destroy! Getting the body of Christ distracted is a strategic plan of the enemy--Delaying the body of Christ from fully awakening. Demonic influences are convincing believers that we have more time; that we need more rest, that we are doing all we can. This is a lie! We are NOT to be resting and just going through life and the motions. It is time to move from puzzled to purpose into our future with the body of Christ--taking our place in the vision of God to bring home His family. There will be casualties but we must concern ourselves with the lives assigned to us that God has opened windows of opportunity for them to join us. We can't fail and lay back down to slumber our purpose and dreams away. We have to get positioned, get connected and get into fulfilling the purpose to which we have been called.

I love the Lord. He saved me, but now what? I will not stop teaching and spreading His Word. I will continue to strive for God's best in my life and I will NOT settle for one day or breath short of fulfilling ALL God has assigned for me to do. When I get to the throne and stand before God, I will have no regrets about things I should have done that God had assigned to me. My prayer has been and continues to be that I not leave this earth until all I was born to do has been completed. THAT is the individual puzzle within the vision. I am not concerned. I am determined! I am not afraid. I am destined! I am not lacking. I am more than a conqueror by the authority given to me by one Christ Jesus who died for me and has set the path ahead that I now follow! I am not sure what will be next but I am sure there is something next coming and I will be ready to connect when that time comes.

There are many subjects I believe need our attention. I don't think I am the only way to understanding a certain area of your life but I believe I can offer a unique perspective. You can go from puzzled to purpose in your marriage and I believe my teacher, the Holy Spirit, has given me some insight to share regarding marriage. This may or may not be in the form of a book. The idea is not what I will be doing but that I will be connected to what needs doing as it pleases my Father. Not to long ago, God began to deal with me concerning couples. This is no surprise to me because I was once told by one of my previous Pastors that God usually uses you where you're at in life. What I mean by that is simply if you are a single mother you typically have what it takes to speak to single moms. If you are a widowed father you may find yourself speaking to other fathers who have lost their spouse. Parents can give advice to other parents and in my case being married allows the Holy Spirit to give me insight in that area. I think one of my theology professors called it the Holy Spirit classroom 101 because that's exactly what it is. You find yourself sitting as a student to the Holy Spirit in a class you didn't necessarily know was on your list of courses. My classroom has been my life and the people God has allowed in it.

My mother will forever be my female hero when it comes to getting the job done. She taught me to be committed to whatever I put my hands to even if that is simply doing the dishes. It took courage for her to be a mother in tough times but she did it. I am currently and forevermore going to be in the study of marriage because that is where God has me and I have a husband who was gifted to me for this purpose. Together we experience God for ourselves and find out new revelations regarding relationships and it is exciting. It is so exciting that we feel it necessary to share in order that God can be exalted in this area specifically. The vision God has placed before us came from writing and processing the strategies within this book. It came from the Holy Spirit revealing to me that there is so much to this idea of connection.

I am so full of purpose simply from taking myself out of the box. This whole thing started almost two years ago when I finally asked myself what I wanted to be when I grew up? I knew I was a Christian. I knew I believed in the things of God but I wanted to know what was next. I had to know. I had experienced some things in my life and had some wonderful experiences with

God but still the need to know Him more and to be closer to Him was aching at my soul. It pushed me to do better and be better and seek after the things of God like never before.

I began to start telling myself yes instead of no. I began to look at the impossible and ask questions of myself like why not. I remember getting a phone call exclaiming that I was eligible for a makeover from the Oprah Winfrey Network. Oprah had just launched her new network and was testing some pilot shows. One of which showcased families in need of a home makeover. I could go on about the details of how Chad (my husband) and myself were selected for the show but that is neither here nor there. The point is, I didn't say no. I said why not. After the makeover and taking a peek behind the scenes of what life is like for people in that kind of industry, I was determined more than ever to keep saying yes and to keep connecting. Maybe God will give me a platform to truly go into detail how many things had to line up for all these things to take place and how awesome God was to my husband and I in the process.

It was a reminder that God cared about the little things in my life and there would be more to come if I kept seeking. Seeking after Him connecting daily with what He had for me. I didn't know who or what form my answers would come so I had to be open to various experiences. This makeover experience in particular introduced us to an eclectic group of worker bees I called them. From all over the country this group of people pulled their skills together, some of them never having met before worked together under pressing circumstances to make our newlywed dreams came true. We were still considered newlyweds at that time. We talked to the electricians, the painters, the designers, camera crew and so forth and gained so much insight as to how important each of their roles really were. This connection thing was happening all around us all the time but as the body of Christ, I'm not sure we truly grasp it the way the world does. This strategic act of grouping together and connecting for a common purpose gets the job done. That to me was a spark!

Almost a year later a friend of mine had won tickets to see Oprah and Bishop T.D. Jakes in St. Louis for her Lifeclass tour. Once again the circumstances that had to work themselves out in order for me to go to this event just lined up. God is good! This particular tour had guest speaker Bishop T.D. Jakes who gave an awesome break down regarding how we as Christians should be living on purpose! Did you catch that? There goes that word again. Purpose. I was getting goose bumps sitting in the audience. You can actually view this on Youtube now and you might get a sneak peek of me in the audience a few times. My friend and I had great seats. I left that event determined to seek out my purpose more than I had ever done before. This time however I wanted to do it God's way. This time I opened myself up to His guidance and His correction so that I could begin this connection process for myself. I began to see where I had missed it. Many times I attempted to figure things out on my own. As you have read some of my stories you may have noticed that I have often felt like an outsider. This is a lie from the enemy that kept me from truly accepting myself. This lie also kept me from believing my piece of the puzzle was valuable to the body of Christ. I love talking about this because I'm passionate about others making this discovery as well. This is not meant to sound as if I have it all figured out and that there is nothing left to discover.

This book was meant to do the complete opposite of that. It is a strategic entry point into the various possibilities God has awaiting you in multiple areas of your life. By all means don't stop here! You can go from puzzled to purpose in your marriage, in your parenting, in your career, in your dreams of ministry. That is exactly what my future holds. I want to write more, do more and be an equipper for the body of Christ, all for the Glory of God. I feel the Father's heartbeat as I write because I know this is near and dear to Him.

He wants you and I to discover not just ONE purpose, but many and to enjoy each one as we journey through life. I'm going to continue on this journey with my husband, my kids, my family and friends. I believe part of my purpose is to be a distributor to others so they are equipped to fulfill the part they play in God's vision for the body of Christ. I also believe that as I grow and I increase in the ability to distribute, God will be magnified as He demonstrates His grace, mercy, power and ultimate love for us. I'm excited! I would love to hear how this book has sparked the strategist in you. Are you on your way from being puzzled about what you want out of life and on your way to purpose?

About the Author

Tasha Hart is the author of Puzzled to Purpose. Establishing herself as a confident speaker, Tasha has completed more than the required number of speeches to reach Confident Communicator status with Toastmaster's International. Organizing community events that promote unity is a strong passion of hers to include the Annual Living Prayer Box. This event involves several volunteers who pray and take prayer requests from a box over the duration of 24 hours. This event, along with preparing 501 (c) 3 paperwork for non-profit organizations to reach their tax exempt status, is just a couple of her accomplishments. Many non-profits credit her for consulting them through the tax-exempt status while helping them achieve a ministry dream of their own. Her heart to help the body of Christ has led her to lead giving efforts in the community, small groups, vacation Bible school activities, teaching Sunday school classes, and other outreach programs. She has taught on live broadcasts through social media on Periscope. Her online teaching topics include inspirational messages founded on Biblical principles that encourage viewers to find their purpose in life. Tasha has been invited to speak at Women's conferences and frequently participates in artistic trade shows that showcase her love and talent for the arts. Equipping the body of Christ is her passion, and this new work will definitely strum those heart strings.

Stay Connected

Thank you for purchasing Secrets of the Twelve. Tasha would love to connect with you. Below are a few ways you can stay up to date on book signings, new book releases, and more!

INSTAGRAM @tashartlife
FACEBOOK tashartlife
PERISCOPE tashartlife
TWITTER @tashartlife
WEBSITE www.tashartlife.com

www.ingramcontent.com/pod-product-compliance
Lightning Source LLC
Chambersburg PA
CBHW060038040426
42331CB00032B/1018